Renewing America's Nuclear Arsenal:
Options for the 21st Century

James E. Doyle

Renewing America's Nuclear Arsenal:
Options for the 21st Century

James E. Doyle

IISS The International Institute for Strategic Studies

The International Institute for Strategic Studies

Arundel House | 6 Temple Place | London | WC2R 2PG | UK

First published September 2017 **Routledge**
4 Park Square, Milton Park, Abingdon, Oxon, OX14 4RN

for **The International Institute for Strategic Studies**
Arundel House, 6 Temple Place, London, WC2R 2PG, UK
www.iiss.org

Simultaneously published in the USA and Canada by **Routledge**
711 Third Avenue, New York, NY 10017

Routledge is an imprint of Taylor & Francis, an Informa Business

© 2017 The International Institute for Strategic Studies

DIRECTOR-GENERAL AND CHIEF EXECUTIVE Dr John Chipman
EDITOR Dr Nicholas Redman
ASSISTANT EDITOR Alice Aveson
EDITORIAL Katherine Carr, Chris Raggett, Gaynor Roberts
COVER/PRODUCTION John Buck, Kelly Verity

The International Institute for Strategic Studies is an independent centre for research, information and debate on the problems of conflict, however caused, that have, or potentially have, an important military content. The Council and Staff of the Institute are international and its membership is drawn from almost 100 countries. The Institute is independent and it alone decides what activities to conduct. It owes no allegiance to any government, any group of governments or any political or other organisation. The IISS stresses rigorous research with a forward-looking policy orientation and places particular emphasis on bringing new perspectives to the strategic debate.

The Institute's publications are designed to meet the needs of a wider audience than its own membership and are available on subscription, by mail order and in good bookshops. Further details at www.iiss.org.

British Library Cataloguing in Publication Data
A catalogue record for this book is available from the British Library

Library of Congress Cataloging in Publication Data

ADELPHI series
ISSN 1944-5571

ADELPHI 462
ISBN 978-0-8153-8466-3

Contents

ALCM	Air-launched cruise missile
CTBT	Comprehensive Nuclear-Test-Ban Treaty (1996)
DoD	US Department of Defense
DoE	US Department of Energy
GBSD	Ground-Based Strategic Deterrent
GLCM	Ground-launched cruise missile
ICBM	Intercontinental ballistic missile
INF Treaty	Treaty Between The United States Of America And The Union Of Soviet Socialist Republics On The Elimination Of Their Intermediate-Range And Shorter-Range Missiles (1987, commonly referred to as the Intermediate-Range Nuclear Forces Treaty)
ISR	Intelligence, surveillance and reconnaissance
IW	Interoperable warhead
JASSM	Joint Air-to-Surface Standoff Missile
JASSM–ER	Joint Air-to-Surface Standoff Missile–Extended Range
JDAM	Joint Direct Attack Munition
JSOW	Joint Standoff Weapon
LEP	Life-extension programme
LRSO	Long-Range Standoff Weapon
MIRV	Multiple independently targetable re-entry vehicle
Mk4-A	Re-entry vehicles of the UGM-133A *Trident* II SLBM that carry the W76 warhead

Mk-5	Re-entry vehicles of the UGM-133A *Trident* II SLBM that carry the W88 warhead
New START	The Treaty between the United States of America and the Russian Federation on Measures for the Further Reduction and Limitation of Strategic Offensive Arms (Strategic Arms Reduction Treaty, 2010)
NNSA	National Nuclear Security Administration
NPR	Nuclear Posture Review
NPT	Treaty on the Non-Proliferation of Nuclear Weapons (1968)
SLBM	Submarine-launched ballistic missile
SSBN	Nuclear-powered ballistic-missile submarine
SSGN	Nuclear-powered guided-missile submarine
SSMP	Stockpile Stewardship and Management Plan
SSN	Nuclear-powered attack submarine

The author wishes to thank the Paul Olum Fellowship at the Ploughshares Fund for supporting research for this book.

In the next few years the government of the United States will make decisions regarding the renewal of its nuclear forces that will have huge implications for the security of the country and its allies, its public finances and the salience of nuclear weapons in global politics. Current plans provide for spending an estimated US$1 trillion over 30 years to modernise or replace the full triad of air-, land- and sea-based nuclear weapons.[1] This would amount to renewing the Cold War-era nuclear arsenal as a central part of US security strategy, rather than restructuring the force in a manner that would acknowledge fundamental changes in the security environment and seek to lead the world in a strategic transition away from nuclear weapons.

While the planned timescale for the complete modernisation or replacement of the triad exceeds 30 years, key decisions on most major weapons-system procurement will occur during the next decade. Most of the current warheads and delivery vehicles will reach the end of their designed operational lifetimes at various points over the next 20 years. Facilities to produce or refurbish nuclear warheads in the enduring stockpile also require modernisation, consolidation and improved safety.

The structure of the US nuclear arsenal (and Russia's) is a hangover from the Cold War, with three major types of delivery platforms: nuclear-missile submarines, land-based ballistic missiles and strategic aircraft. If the New START Treaty, signed by the US and the Russian Federation in 2010, is fully implemented by 5 February 2018, both nations will possess strategic nuclear forces of approximately 1,550 'accountable' nuclear warheads. The actual number of deployed warheads may be closer to 2,000, because under the treaty formula strategic aircraft are counted as carrying one warhead, when in reality they can and do carry more.[2] Both countries will also retain several thousand reserve nuclear warheads and non-strategic warheads that are not covered under the New START Treaty.[3]

The current US modernisation plans call for the construction of a new triad of nuclear-weapons systems over the next 20–30 years – effectively replicating the full range of existing systems – which will remain in service until 2080 or later. The planned new weapons and delivery systems include 100 new B-21 *Raider* strategic aircraft, 1,000–1,100 new nuclear-armed cruise missiles, 12 new *Columbia*-class strategic ballistic-missile submarines and 400 new land-based intercontinental ballistic missiles (ICBMs). In addition, the US plans to refurbish seven types of nuclear warheads. Plans for each leg of the nuclear triad under these plans and their estimated costs are summarised in Table 1.

The current plans, and the purposes and uses for US nuclear weapons are articulated in official documents including the 2010 Nuclear Posture Review (NPR), the 2012 Department of Defense (DoD) document 'Sustaining U.S. Global Leadership: Priorities for 21st Century Defense', the 2013 Report on Nuclear Employment Strategy, the 2014 Quadrennial Defense Review and the 2015 National Security Strategy of the United States.[4] The Congressional Budget Office has estimated that

Table 1: **Estimated costs of US nuclear-modernisation plan**[7]

Triad elements	Weapon	Plan	Number requested	FY2017 request	Overall cost estimate
Air	Long-Range Standoff Weapon (LRSO)	New	1,000–1,100	US$95.6m	US$20bn–30bn
	B-21 (long-range strike bomber)	New	80–100	US$1.35bn	US$60bn–80bn
	B61-12 (guided gravity bomb)	Modification	400–500	US$137.9m	US$12bn
	W80-4 (warhead)	Life extension	N/A	US$220.3m	US$7.1bn–9.7bn
Sea	Columbia (nuclear submarine)	New	12	US$1.86bn	US$139bn
	Trident II (missile)	Modification	N/A	US$1.22bn	US$6bn
	W88 (warhead)	Life extension	N/A	US$281.3m	US$3bn–4bn
	W76-1 (warhead)	Life extension	N/A	US$222.9m	US$4.4bn
Air + Sea	Interoperable warheads (IW-1–3)	Modification	N/A	N/A	US$48.4bn–71.2bn
Ground	Ground-Based Strategic Deterrent (GBSD) programme: Minuteman ICBM replacement	New	642 (400 deployed)	US$113.9m	US$62bn

Sources: US Department of Defense; National Nuclear Security Administration; Congressional Research Service

programmes supporting the modernisation or replacement of the US nuclear triad during 2017–26 will cost US$400 billion, an average of US$40bn a year.[5] Other studies have projected that the cost of nuclear-forces modernisation over the 30-year period will be approximately US$1 trillion, with more recent estimates exceeding that sum.[6]

Each of the nuclear-weapon delivery systems described in Table 1 is fitted with nuclear warheads. This includes warheads designed for delivery by ballistic or cruise missiles, and unpowered nuclear bombs dropped from aircraft. In September 2009 the United States announced that its nuclear arsenal contained 5,113 warheads.[8]

In early 2015, experts estimated that the nuclear stockpile of the US DoD had been reduced to 4,760 warheads. This constitutes the military stockpile of nuclear weapons theoretically available to the US for use in warfare. Approximately 2,080 of these nuclear weapons are deployed, meaning that they are on or near the missiles or aircraft that can deliver them to a target within minutes or hours. Another 2,680 warheads are in storage. In addition to the warheads in DoD custody, approximately 2,340 retired but still intact warheads are in storage in the custody of the Department of Energy (DoE) awaiting dismantlement, making a total US inventory of roughly 7,100 warheads.[9]

What price deterrence?

Alternative force structures would meet the criteria for a US nuclear force at a lower cost. A modernised force of 1,550 deployed nuclear warheads, as permitted by New START and ample to deter threats against the US and its allies from nuclear-armed rivals, can be purchased and maintained for far less than the US$1 trillion 30-year plan envisioned by former president Barack Obama's fiscal year 2017 budget and upheld by initial budgets proposed by the Trump administration. The DoD's 2013 Report on Nuclear Employment Strategy concluded that a force of 1,000–1,100 deployed nuclear weapons could meet all deterrence needs, even allowing for planned modernisation of Russia and China's nuclear forces. Downsizing the US force to these levels by 2030 could save additional hundreds of billions of dollars.

Meeting US deterrence needs with a smaller, cheaper nuclear arsenal creates a range of opportunities. For instance, it would obviate the need to cut back major conventional-weapons procurement and non-military national-security expenditure.[10] Annual costs for planned nuclear-weapons modernisation alone, at US$40bn, could support 20–25 new active-duty army combat brigades or double the navy's annual shipbuilding budget. For US$20bn per year, which is half of what is required for current nuclear-modernisation plans, the US Air Force could buy and operate more than 40 new F-22 fighter aircraft or 2,200 armed MQ-9 *Reaper* drones annually.

A reduced-size arsenal would also give impetus to new and existing arms-control initiatives. China, France, Russia, the United Kingdom and the US remain obligated by their commitments under the 1968 Treaty on the Non-Proliferation of Nuclear Weapons (NPT) to seek the eventual elimination of nuclear weapons. A step in that direction by the US would go some way towards assuaging the frustration of dozens of non-nuclear-weapon states at the failure of the five acknowledged nuclear powers to make good on their treaty commitments.

Nuclear weapons do not provide the US or its allies with protection from terrorism, regional conflict, humanitarian crises, environmental degradation or outbreaks of disease. Technological advancement in computing, sensor technology and unmanned systems are making traditional basing of nuclear weapons more vulnerable. The possession of nuclear weapons – especially in large numbers and at a high readiness – already presents an existential threat to all nations. Nuclear weapons could be used by accident or miscalculation. Furthermore, large, geographically dispersed nuclear forces provide non-state actors with opportunities for sabotage or theft. Silo-based ICBMs are already vulnerable to direct or cyber attack.

The purpose of this book is to demonstrate that there are alternatives to the current plan for nuclear-force modernisation. These alternatives would allow the US to maintain deterrence at a lower cost, thereby freeing up funds to ease pressing shortfalls in spending on conventional procurement and nuclear security. Moreover, alternative structures – which propose changes to both the size and shape of the US arsenal – offer distinct advantages over the existing plan with regard to maintaining strategic stability vis-à-vis Russia and China; upholding existing arms-control treaties, in particular New START and the Intermediate-Range Nuclear Forces (INF) Treaty; and boosting the security of US nuclear forces and supporting the global non-proliferation regime, including the NPT. They would also endow the US with a nuclear force better suited to the strategic environment of the twenty-first century, and mark an advance on the existing triad with regard to supporting conventional military operations.

The purposes of the US nuclear arsenal

When assessing alternatives to the existing plan for modernisation, it is essential to consider the main purposes of the US nuclear arsenal and other objectives it must meet. The principal function of the force is to deter a range of plausible threats from nuclear-armed rivals against the US and its allies. To achieve this, the US must possess a nuclear force that can survive a first strike and still reliably deliver a devastating response that metes out unacceptable damage to an adversary. Provided that an adversary is convinced of both the United States' capability and will to retaliate with devastating effect, it will be deterred from attacking the US or its allies with nuclear weapons. Properly configured, nuclear forces also contribute to deterring conventional attacks, but are far less effective at this than deterring nuclear attacks.

Nuclear forces must also be reliable and provide the US president with diverse options for responding to the threat or use of nuclear weapons. These options range from discriminate attacks on the enemy's military targets that limit collateral damage, to massive attacks on urban areas and economic infrastructure. Although the 2013 Report on Nuclear Employment Strategy suggests that deterrence needs can be met with 1,000–1,100 deployed nuclear warheads, none of the official public documents state how many and what types of nuclear weapons are needed to deter a 'range of plausible threats'.

Debate continues on the question of 'how much is enough?' Some assert that the complexity of the future security environment and the nuclear-weapon modernisation programmes of Russia, China and North Korea require the US to replace its entire triad of nuclear-delivery vehicles and deploy 1,500 warheads or more, as permitted under New START, and perhaps to increase the force after the treaty expires in February 2021. Voices on this side of the debate believe robust nuclear forces are essential for long-term deterrence, are affordable, and provide the US with means to effectively influence the strategic decisions of adversaries and allies. They typically downplay the risk that nuclear forces could be used by accident or miscalculation, or stolen by terrorists. They view such risks as justifiable, acceptable or manageable, given the nature of threats in the international system and the fact that potential adversaries are likely to retain their nuclear weapons for the foreseeable future.

A contrary view, espoused by a group of analysts and former policymakers, questions the enduring value of nuclear weapons for US, allied and global security in the coming decades.[11] Some of them support a fundamentally different perception of the risks and benefits of maintaining nuclear weapons as a central feature of US national-security strategy. They view nuclear deterrence as a fragile means of preventing nuclear war; prone to unpredictability, accident, and human and mechanical error that could trigger an unintended and catastrophic nuclear war. Among them is former president Obama, who declared in 2009 that his administration would work towards the 'peace and security of a world without nuclear weapons' and favour progress towards that goal in the decades ahead.[12]

This side of the debate takes seriously the risk that terrorists or non-state actors could acquire or sabotage nuclear weapons, and so favours reducing the size of nuclear stockpiles and spending more to improve their security.[13] It holds that deterrence can be achieved with fewer nuclear weapons and lower costs, enabling the US to better fund other defence priorities.[14] The security of nuclear weapons in the face of possible theft or sabotage by state or non-state actors is indeed a vital consideration for the US government, along with the impact that its arsenal has on the global effort to check the proliferation of nuclear weapons, including through the NPT. It is widely accepted that the further global spread of nuclear weapons increases the chances that they could be used in conflict and that terrorists could acquire them. The threat of US retaliation would do little to deter a terrorist group from using nuclear weapons, were it to acquire them.

As a concomitant to securing effective deterrence, the size and structure of the nuclear force should contribute to the maintenance of strategic stability in relations between the US and the other principal nuclear powers. This concerns both stability in a crisis situation and with regard to procurement that could trigger a nuclear-arms race. It also concerns the fate of arms-control treaties to which the US is a signatory.

The final set of considerations bearing on the nuclear-modernisation decision concerns the role of nuclear forces within the US military, in particular the opportunity costs of the nuclear force and the extent to which it contributes to conventional military operations. If the US has US$200bn to spend annually on weapons (as opposed to military salaries, health care and pensions), spending US$40bn annually on nuclear forces when US$10bn would be sufficient for deterrence constitutes a catastrophic misallocation of resources, with negative implications for US security across the board. Moreover, given the enormous cost of the nuclear force, it is advantageous for defence planners if that force can contribute to conventional operations as well as performing deterrence missions.

Alternative force configurations

This book puts forward three alternative plans for nuclear-force modernisation and compares them with the existing plan. Many different permutations are possible with regard to the number and type of platforms procured, the warheads placed on them and way they are deployed. The three alternatives, summarised in Table 2, give a sense of the range of options available.

Option 1 calls for a slimmer or 'streamlined' triad of nuclear weapons, comprising eight new *Columbia* nuclear-powered ballistic-missile submarines (SSBNs) instead of 12, and 300 replacement ICBMs instead of 400. The 100-strong strategic-bomber force, and the weapons it would carry, are unchanged from the default plan. This alternative would comply with New START, supporting 1,100–1,500 operationally deployed strategic warheads according to the treaty's counting rules.

Option 2 would eliminate ICBMs entirely from 2030, relying on ten *Columbia*-class SSBNs and 80 B-21 strategic bombers, albeit without a new nuclear cruise missile and with the new B61-12 nuclear bomb retained in the US rather than deployed to Europe. This 'air–sea dyad' force could field up to 1,100 operationally deployed strategic warheads depending on submarine-launched ballistic-missile (SLBM) warhead loading.

Option 3 would also eliminate the ICBM element from 2030, and relies on a new fleet of 80 B-21 aircraft without a new nuclear-armed cruise missile or the deployment of the B61-12 bombs in Europe. The nuclear missiles on the seaborne aspect of this dyad are distributed more widely, on a combination of six *Columbia*-class SSBNs and eight *Virginia*-class nuclear-

Table 2: **Alternative nuclear-modernisation plans**

	Current plans: Full triad	Option 1: Streamlined triad	Option 2: Air–sea dyad	Option 3: Dispersed maritime dyad
Strategic bombers/ cruise missiles	100 B-21/ 1,000 LRSO	100 B-21/ 1,000 LRSO	80 B-21/ 0 LRSO	80 B-21/ 0 LRSO
ICBMs	400 *Minuteman* III replacements	300 *Minuteman* III replacements	0	0
Nuclear submarines/ SLBMs	12 *Columbia*/16 SLBMs each	8 *Columbia*/16 SLBMs each	10 *Columbia*/16 SLBMs each	6 *Columbia*/16 SLBMs each 8 *Virginia*/4 SLBMs each
Non-strategic nuclear forces	B61-12 deployed with NATO	B61-12 deployed with NATO	B61-12 produced but not deployed to NATO	B61-12 produced but not deployed to NATO
Total New START-accountable warheads[a]	1,550	1,100–1,500	1,100 or fewer	750

[a] In all four cases, the proposed nuclear-force structure would be capable of delivering more nuclear warheads than the New START numbers because the treaty counts strategic bombers as one warhead when each bomber can in fact carry 10–20 nuclear weapons.

powered attack submarines (SSNs) that would be modified to carry ballistic missiles. This 'dispersed maritime dyad' force would support almost 1,000 operationally deployed strategic warheads, although under New START counting rules the number would be 750.

The two dyad options in particular could provide significant cost savings over the life cycle of the nuclear stockpile and its production infrastructure. Both allow for the retirement of the W78 and W87 ICBM warheads and the W80 cruise-missile warhead, eliminating the need for life-extension programmes for these weapons or the so-called 'interoperable warheads' envisioned by the DoE's 3+2 stockpile strategy for use on both SLBMs and ICBMs.[15]

Implementing the existing plan or any of the alternatives is a 20–30 year undertaking. Any of the four options would provide the US with a large, diverse, flexible and responsive nuclear arsenal that would give the president multiple options for employing nuclear weapons. Hundreds of nuclear warheads of varying destructive yield (from a fraction of a kiloton to more than 400 kilotons) would be available for use even if the US suffered an attack by Russia, its strongest potential adversary.

All of the force structures would provide the means for limited and discriminate nuclear strikes in any global region. In addition, at very low levels of nuclear employment by adversaries with small nuclear forces (between one and three nuclear weapons of less than 20 kilotons), the US retains and is dramatically expanding its ability to strike effectively and limit damage with missile defences and non-nuclear weapons. Only in extreme circumstances would a nuclear response be required for an attack of this scale. One such circumstance would be if the attacker retained additional nuclear weapons that could not be destroyed by conventional means. However, after any nuclear use, re-establishing deterrence and avoiding nuclear escalation would be in the national-security interest of the US and its allies. This highlights the need to increase the capabilities of non-nuclear forces.

All four proposed modernisation plans also provide the capability for a rapid expansion in the number of deliverable warheads, should changes in the security environment call for it. This can be done by adding additional warheads to inter-continental missiles and deploying reserve aircraft-delivered weapons currently in storage.

This book argues that the US can transition to a deployed nuclear arsenal and stockpile at or below New START levels that meet anticipated deterrence needs, while improving strategic stability, nuclear security and non-proliferation, as well as saving billions of dollars, thus avoiding painful cuts to conventional procurement or other areas of federal government spending. One of the alternatives, moreover, would result in a nuclear force that is better able to support conventional missions.

CHAPTER ONE

The plan for a trillion-dollar triad

The US plans to renew its nuclear triad – its fleet of nuclear bombers, ballistic-missile submarines, and land-based ICBMs and their nuclear warheads – in full in the coming years. The airborne part of the nuclear force will retain some B-52 and B-2 bombers but will largely consist of 100 new B-21 strategic aircraft (although not all of them may be produced for nuclear missions), equipped with more than 1,000 new nuclear-armed cruise missiles as well as upgraded bombs. The land-based leg will consist of 400 new ICBMs to replace the existing *Minuteman* III missiles. The seaborne leg of the triad will rest on 12 new *Columbia*-class SSBNs. Seven types of nuclear warhead will be part of the nuclear arsenal in support of these new delivery platforms.

Strategic aircraft and cruise missiles

In October 2015 the US Air Force awarded a contract to procure a new, nuclear-armed, long-range penetrating strike bomber (designated the B-21 *Raider*) to Northrop Grumman. It is estimated that the 100 new aircraft ordered will cost in excess of US$80bn and enter service from 2025,[1] with production potentially continuing beyond 2030. It is uncertain how many of these new strategic aircraft will be equipped for nuclear missions.

As the new B-21 aircraft are delivered, the older B-52 and B-1 bombers will be retired, although some of these planes will remain in service until 2040 or beyond, as will the 20 B-2 strategic aircraft. The current plans call for the B-21 aircraft to be equipped to carry the B61-12 guided nuclear bomb and a new long-range nuclear-armed cruise missile (currently designated the Long-Range Standoff Weapon–LRSO). If the new B-21 bombers are available as planned in 2025, they may be equipped with the existing AGM-86B nuclear air-launched cruise missile (ALCM) until that missile is retired sometime after 2030 and replaced by the LRSO.[2]

The proposed LRSO nuclear-armed cruise missile is the second major procurement programme for the air-breathing leg of the nuclear triad in the next 30 years. Current plans call for the acquisition of 1,000–1,100 missiles at a projected cost of US$9bn (the nuclear warhead for these missiles will cost at least US$10bn–15bn). The new missiles are to enter service in 2025 and remain operational for at least 30 years. Full-scale development is planned to begin in 2017, with US$1.8bn allocated up to 2020.[3]

Land-based ICBMs

The US land-based ICBM force currently consists of 450 *Minuteman* III ICBMs, each deployed with one warhead. By early February 2018 the fleet will decline to 400 deployed missiles, while retaining all 450 launchers, in accordance with the New START Treaty. The Air Force has also undertaken a modernisation programme for the *Minuteman* III missiles, replacing and upgrading their rocket motors, guidance systems and other components, to extend their service lives until 2030.[4]

The current modernisation plans call for the replacement of 400 *Minuteman* III nuclear ICBMs with new missiles, beginning in 2027. A preliminary estimate completed in February 2015 by the Air Force Nuclear Weapons Center's ICBM System Program Office put the acquisition cost of the *Minuteman* III replacement system – an option studied under the Pentagon's Ground-Based Strategic Deterrent (GBSD) programme – at US$62.3bn,[5] covering a 30-year period between the fiscal years 2015 and 2044. Debate continues on the actual cost of the ICBM replacement plan, with some estimates as high as US$120bn for the new missiles.[6] The 2015 cost estimates for the GBSD programme have already been revised upwards. The Pentagon's Office of Cost Assessment and Program Evaluation in May 2017 produced a low-end estimate of US$85bn to replace the *Minuteman* III ICBMs, more than one-third higher than the Air Force's figure.[7]

The Air Force completed an analysis of alternatives for the ICBM force that was briefed to industry officials in July 2014. It plans to maintain the basic design of the *Minuteman* III, its communications system and launch silos, but would replace the rocket motors, guidance sets, post-boost vehicles and re-entry systems. This means the Air Force would effectively deploy a new missile in the current *Minuteman* infrastructure. Reports also indicate that, although this missile would be deployed in fixed silos, the design would allow it to be deployed on mobile launchers in the future, a basing mode that would add significant cost.

Ballistic-missile submarines

The US Navy is currently conducting development and design work on the new *Columbia* class of ballistic-missile submarines. This new submarine is planned to replace the *Ohio*-class *Trident* nuclear submarines as they reach the end of their service lives from 2027. However, it is estimated that the first new vessel will enter the fleet in 2031, meaning that the number of SSBNs is expected to decline to ten for most of the 2030s. The Navy is designing the new submarines with only 16 ballistic-missile launch tubes as part of cost-saving efforts. The *Trident* submarines have 24 launch tubes, and each currently carries 24 missiles, although the Navy plans to reduce this to 20 on each submarine by the end of 2017 as the US downsizes its forces to comply with New START.

The Navy has estimated that, in 2014 dollars, the 12-boat *Columbia* fleet will cost US$139bn. It expects the first submarine to cost US$14.5bn, comprising US$8.8bn in construction costs and US$5.7bn in non-recurring engineering work. Subsequent submarines are expected to cost US$9.8bn.[8]

Nuclear warheads

The US nuclear-weapons stockpile is composed of seven different types of warhead. Current plans call for the modernisation (life extension) of several of these types during the next 20–40 years. The US DoE's National Nuclear Security Administration (NNSA) conducts this work in its network of national laboratories and production sites. The costs of nuclear-warhead maintenance and modernisation must be added to the DoD's nuclear-weapons expenditure to calculate the total cost of US nuclear forces. US nuclear warheads, associated delivery vehicles and major nuclear-warhead life-extension programmes (LEPs) are described in Table 3.

The air-breathing leg of the triad (bombers and cruise missiles) carries variants of the B61 and B83 nuclear bombs on aircraft and the W80 nuclear warhead on nuclear-armed cruise missiles. An LEP is underway for the B61 bomb family and is planned for the W80 cruise-missile warhead.

Approximately 400 B61-12 nuclear bombs are being modernised to replace three previous versions of the bomb

Table 3: **US nuclear warheads and associated delivery systems**

Type[a]	Description	Delivery system	Mission	Planned life-extension programme 2015–39
W78	Re-entry vehicle warhead	*Minuteman* III ICBM	Surface to surface	X
W87	Re-entry vehicle warhead	*Minuteman* III ICBM	Surface to surface	X
W76-0/1	Re-entry body warhead	*Trident* II D-5 SLBM	Underwater to surface	X
W88	Re-entry body warhead	*Trident* II D-5 SLBM	Underwater to surface	X
B61-3/4/10	Non-strategic bombs Replaced by B61-12	F-15, F-16, certified NATO aircraft	Air to surface	X
B61-7	Strategic bomb	B-52 and B-2 bombers	Air to surface	
B61-11	Strategic bomb	B-2 bomber	Air to surface	
B83-1	Strategic bomb	B-52 and B-2 bombers	Air to surface	
W80-1	Air-launched cruise missile strategic weapon	B-52 bomber	Air to surface	X

[a] The suffix associated with a warhead or bomb type ('-0/1' for the W76, for example) represents the modification associated with the respective weapon.

Source: NNSA FY2017 Stockpile Stewardship and Management Plan, pp. 1–3, https://nnsa.energy.gov/ourmission/managingthestockpile/ssmp

(modifications 3, 4 and 10). The first new B61-12 bombs are scheduled to enter service in 2020. The costs of the B61 programme have risen sharply: the DoE initially claimed that it would cost around US$4bn, but estimates now range from US$9.5bn to US$12bn, making it the most expensive nuclear-warhead programme in US history.[9] The B61-7, B61-11 and B83 nuclear bombs will be retired as the B61-12 is deployed. The modernised cruise-missile warhead, designated the W80-4, is planned for deployment on the new LRSO cruise missile from 2027. The NNSA's FY2016 Stockpile Stewardship and Management Plan (SSMP) estimates that the W80-4 programme will cost US$5.8bn–7.8bn (in FY2015 dollars).[10]

Warhead LEPs are also planned for the ICBM and SLBM legs of the triad. The first of these, the W76 SLBM warhead LEP, is more than 50% complete. The W76 warhead arms most of the *Trident* II D-5 SLBMs on the US *Ohio*-class submarines. Approximately 800–900 modernised W76-1 warheads have been delivered to the Navy, with around 800 more to be upgraded by 2019. The primary goals of the W76-1 LEP are to extend the original warhead service life from 20 to 60 years, address identified ageing issues, incorporate nuclear-surety enhancements and minimise system-certification risk in the absence of underground nuclear testing. The estimated cost of the W76 LEP is US$3.7bn.

The second SLBM warhead undergoing refurbishment is the W88. The W88 entered the stockpile in late 1988 and is also deployed on the Navy's *Trident* II D-5 SLBM system. Current plans call for an alteration (Alt) to the warhead prior to a full LEP. The W88 Alt 370 replaces the Arming Fusing & Firing subsystem, enhances nuclear safety and supports future alternatives for nuclear-explosive package LEPs. The Nuclear

Figure 1: **NNSA's 3+2 warhead-life-extension schedule[a]**

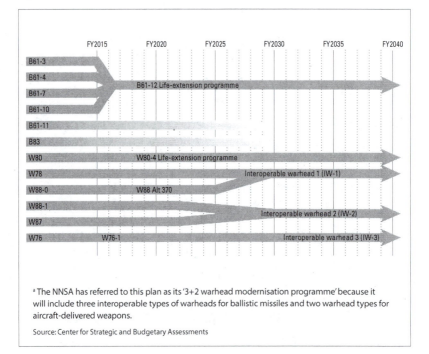

[a] The NNSA has referred to this plan as its '3+2 warhead modernisation programme' because it will include three interoperable types of warheads for ballistic missiles and two warhead types for aircraft-delivered weapons.

Source: Center for Strategic and Budgetary Assessments

Table 4: **Costs and dates of planned warhead-life-extension programmes**

Warhead	Programme dates	Cost estimate (FY2015, US$ billion)
W76-1	FY2010–FY2020	3.7
B61-12	FY2014–FY2020	8
W88 Alt 370	FY2013–FY2020	3.7
W80-4	FY2016–FY2030	7.8
IW-1	FY2020–FY2043	14.9
IW-2	FY2023–FY2049	15.3
IW-3	FY2023–FY2049	14.2
		Total: US$67.6bn

Weapons Council approved the W88 Alt 370 on 9 October 2012. The W88 Alt 370 first production unit is scheduled for 2020 and will keep the W88 in service until the late 2030s, when it is scheduled for a full LEP. The estimated cost of the W88 Alt 370 programme is US$3.7bn.

The NNSA has announced plans to produce modernised 'interoperable' warheads that can be carried by either ICBMs or SLBMs. The FY2016 SSMP states that 'Consolidation of the present four ballistic missile systems (warheads) into three interoperable systems (warheads) will enable an eventual reduction in the number of weapons retained in the stockpile as a hedge against technical failure.'[11]

The first modernised interoperable warhead is planned to be a combined design to replace the W78 ICBM warhead and the W88 SLBM warhead (see Figure 1). The new warhead will be designated 'interoperable warhead (IW)-1'. IW-1 will be followed by IW-2, replacing the W87 ICBM warhead, and IW-3, replacing the W76 SLBM warhead. When the programme is complete there will be three modernised IW warheads that can be placed as needed on either ICBMs or SLBMs. This will allow the retirement of the two current ICBM warheads (W78 and W87) and the two SLBM warheads (W76 and W88). The IW-1 programme is scheduled to begin in 2020, and IW-2 in 2023. Cost estimates are shown in Table 4.

Nuclear-weapons infrastructure

The nuclear-weapons infrastructure, also called the nuclear-weapons complex, is composed of the NNSA Headquarters, NNSA field offices, nuclear-weapons production facilities, national-security laboratories and the Nevada National Security Site (see Figure 2). A highly trained workforce – consisting of federal employees, contractors and assigned members of the military – works at these locations to implement the NNSA's nuclear-weapons mission. NNSA Headquarters develops the plans and coordinates activities to ensure that its strategy to provide nuclear weapons is being accomplished in an efficient and fiscally responsible manner.

The nuclear-weapons manufacturing infrastructure is set to receive two major new facilities, each of which will cost several billion dollars. Controversy surrounds these plans, with many observers disputing both the need for new facilities in order to maintain the nuclear stockpile and the estimated costs that have risen sharply in the past decade. The two facilities are new

Figure 2: **US nuclear-weapons infrastructure**

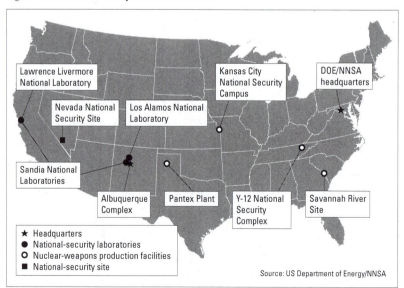

Lawrence Livermore National Laboratory

Kansas City National Security Campus

DOE/NNSA headquarters

Nevada National Security Site

Los Alamos National Laboratory

Sandia National Laboratories

Albuquerque Complex

Pantex Plant

Y-12 National Security Complex

Savannah River Site

★ Headquarters
● National-security laboratories
○ Nuclear-weapons production facilities
■ National-security site

Source: US Department of Energy/NNSA

pit-production buildings at Los Alamos National Laboratory (LANL) in New Mexico and a new Uranium-Processing Facility (UPF) at Oak Ridge National Laboratory in Tennessee.

The NNSA recently approved a four-part plan for establishing a long-term manufacturing capability for producing plutonium pits (cores), the nuclear triggers for thermonuclear weapons, at LANL, in order to meet a congressional mandate for developing an annual production capacity of 50–80 plutonium pits a year by 2030.[12] This represents a significant increase on a rate of approximately 11 pits per year achieved by LANL in August 2011, when it delivered 29 plutonium pits fully certified for use as replacements in the W88 warhead. The plan calls for moving some plutonium work from an older structure to the new Radiological Laboratory Utility Office Building, upgrading the production capacity of the existing Plutonium Facility-4, and two modular additions to the main plutonium-processing facility, known as Technical Area (TA)-55. This new space would house equipment for the pit production and certification process.

This plan is an alternative to a previous proposal to construct a new Chemistry and Metallurgy Research Replacement (CMRR-NF) nuclear facility at Los Alamos. This project was deferred for five years after its budget ballooned from less than US$1bn to more than US$6bn.[13] The FY2017 federal budget request indicates that the alternative plans to the CMRR-NF will cost at least as much and probably more.

At the core of these new plans is the controversial congressional requirement on pit production. There is no clear military justification for a rate of 50–80 pits per year by 2030. In other words, if pits last at least 150 years, for the foreseeable future they will not 'wear out' and need to be replaced at anywhere near this rate in the active stockpile, and there is no rationale for expanding production capacity beyond the current annual rate of 10–20. A production capacity of 50 per year would suffice even if the NNSA found that pits would last only 100 years and that all needed to be replaced by 2089.[14]

The second major facility needed for the SSMP is the new UPF, currently known as the Y-12 plant at Oak Ridge. The current facility was constructed as part of the Manhattan Project during the Second World War. The original projected cost for a new facility was US$1bn and operations were expected to begin as early as FY2013. However, cost estimates for the new facility have soared and its schedule has slipped by several years. The price tag for the facility, renamed the Uranium Capabilities Replacement Project, is now US$6.5bn–19bn.[15]

CHAPTER TWO

Deterrence and flexibility

The principal function of the US nuclear force is to deter a range of plausible threats from nuclear-armed rivals against the US and its allies. This objective is met by keeping high-value targets of potential nuclear adversaries constantly at risk, and by holding nuclear forces that are rapidly employable in a crisis, and able to survive an initial attack and then respond with devastating effect. Nuclear forces must also provide the US president with diverse options for responding to the threat or use of nuclear weapons. These options range from discriminate attacks on the military targets of the enemy that limit collateral damage, to massive attacks on urban areas and economic infrastructure. The US nuclear triad has maintained these attributes for decades. Each leg of the triad can independently deliver hundreds of nuclear weapons with a variety of explosive yields against protected or 'hardened' military targets as well as population centres and economic infrastructure.

US nuclear forces are not intended to threaten states that do not possess nuclear weapons, are party to the 1968 NPT and comply with their nuclear non-proliferation obligations. However, the 2010 NPR stated that the US 'is not prepared at the present time to adopt a universal policy that deterring nuclear attack is the sole purpose of nuclear weapons, but will work to establish conditions under which such a policy could be safely adopted'.[1] The language in the 2010 NPR was qualified in this manner because the US retains the right to use its nuclear weapons not simply for deterring nuclear attacks but also for possible pre-emptive nuclear attacks against potential adversaries. Two situations illustrate this possibility. Firstly, if the US concluded that an adversary was about to launch a nuclear attack on its territory or that of an ally, it could strike first with nuclear weapons in order to prevent that attack or limit the damage. Secondly, if US decision-makers determined that a nation possessing biological or chemical weapons was about to use them, a US pre-emptive nuclear strike could likewise be initiated.

To deter a plausible range of nuclear threats, US nuclear forces must possess attributes and capabilities that convince any potential enemy that the adverse consequences of attacking the US or its allies and partners far outweigh any potential benefit they may seek to gain through an attack.[2] This is a logical objective, but the means to achieve it cannot be known or tested. No one can determine precisely the size, capabilities or posture of a nuclear force that potential adversaries will find convincing. This is because there is no firm understanding of the thought processes and judgements that lead potential adversaries to either refrain from or initiate actions that might lead to conflict or nuclear use. The details or outcome of their cost-benefit analysis cannot be known prior to their actions.

Traditionally, the US has navigated this dilemma by maintaining invulnerable and flexible nuclear forces capable of inflicting what it regards as 'unacceptable damage' on the elements of national power valued by potential adversaries. These elements include military forces (nuclear forces in particular), population, war-supporting industry, critical infrastructure, economic targets and the political leadership.[3]

Conventional wisdom regarding requirements for nuclear-forces modernisation deems that a nuclear force structure that can deliver many hundreds of nuclear weapons of various characteristics to a broad range of targets against the most powerful of US potential adversaries will be sufficient to meet the deterrence criterion. This is consistent with the 2010 NPR and the conclusion of the 2013 Report on Nuclear Employment Strategy, which suggests that deterrence needs can be met with 1,000–1,100 deployed nuclear warheads. Thus for the purposes of this book, 1,000–1,100 warheads are regarded as sufficient to achieve deterrence. However, none of the official public nuclear-strategy documents specifically state what quantity and types of nuclear weapons are needed to deter a 'range of plausible threats'. Great debate continues within the nuclear-planning communities in the US and NATO regarding the specific numbers, characteristics and basing modes of nuclear weapons required for deterrence. As mentioned above, this is because the question of what deters particular adversaries at particular times and places cannot be definitively answered.

The 2013 Report on Nuclear Employment Strategy determined that the existing US arsenal is more than adequate for what the US needs to fulfil its national-security objectives, including deterrence, and that there was no targeting analysis requiring an arsenal in excess of 1,100 warheads. Furthermore, the report drew its conclusions based on current and projected Russian force levels. Given the downturn in US–Russian relations since 2013, this conclusion may be revised in the forthcoming NPR planned by the Trump administration to be concluded by January 2018.

The full triad (current plan)

The US government's existing plan for nuclear modernisation, to maintain an improved, full-strength triad, provides ample, if not excessive, means to deter a range of plausible threats against the US and its allies from nuclear-armed rivals. A replacement force for the *Ohio*-class SSBNs, consisting of 12 *Columbia*-class submarines with 16 SLBMs each, provides a reliable, flexible and survivable system capable of launching hundreds of accurate, powerful nuclear warheads that can destroy civilian or military targets. The *Trident* II missiles the new submarines will carry can deliver up to eight nuclear warheads each. This means that the future submarine leg of the triad alone can deliver nearly 1,000 warheads, depending on warhead loadings on each missile and the number of submarines at sea.

The full triad option also calls for the replacement of the 400 *Minuteman* III ICBMs, starting in 2030. They offer a similar and overlapping capability to the SLBMs but with nearly all missiles ready for prompt launch. Both ICBMs and SLBMs can destroy adversary missile silos and other hardened military targets. Each *Minuteman* III missile carries a single warhead, having previously carried three. No treaty restricts how many warheads each missile could carry, so a future ICBM force could carry 400 warheads on 400 missiles or some other mix of more warheads and fewer missiles.[4] As long as accountable warhead and launcher totals comply with the New START Treaty, the warhead distribution among ICBMs and SLBMs is at the discretion of the US.

Under the full triad option, the air-breathing leg will be modernised to significantly enhance US capabilities to deliver a variety of nuclear and conventional weapons in both strategic and regional scenarios. Planned improvements to this leg will provide tactical flexibility and enhanced capability to defeat or penetrate enemy air defences and destroy mobile and relocatable targets. The crews of new and upgraded strategic aircraft will have the ability to network with space-based early-warning and battle-management sensors and with more tactical aircraft such as F-35 fighters, as well as drones, decoys and cruise missiles.

Redundancy is planned for the air-breathing leg in terms of the capability to promptly attack counterforce targets. Ongoing upgrades to the B-52 and B-2 aircraft will keep some of them in service until 2040 and 2055 respectively. The upgrades include the capability to deliver a variety of weapons from stand-off distances, beyond the range of enemy air defences.

The comprehensive B-2 upgrades will fit out the aircraft with capability to deliver the B61-12 guided bomb and planned LRSO cruise missile with its modernised W80-4 warhead. The B-2 will also carry the B61-11, a high-yield nuclear bomb designed with earth-penetration capabilities, until that weapon is retired in 2025. An estimated 1,000 nuclear weapons, including 528 air-launched cruise missiles, and some very high-yield (1,200 kilotons) B83 bombs are assigned to the B-52 and B-2 bombers.

Alongside their nuclear armaments, the B-52 and B-2 bombers will be equipped to carry a wide range of conventional weapons. These include precision-guided 2,000lb (907kg) Joint Direct Attack Munitions (JDAM); 5,000lb (2267kg) JDAMs; Joint Standoff Weapons (JSOW); Joint Air-to-Surface Standoff Missiles–Extended-Range (JASSM–ER); and 5,000lb GBU-28 'bunker-buster' weapons, among others. The B-2 can also carry a 30,000lb (13,607kg) conventional bomb known as the Massive Ordnance Penetrator, which is designed to defeat deeply buried hard targets.[5]

According to aerospace industry advocate Loren Thompson, from 2025 the new B-21 will provide a new generation of strike and battle-management capabilities in addition to the improved B-2 and B-52 aircraft for both nuclear and conventional warfare. The B-21 is being designed to hold any target on Earth at risk, including deeply buried and mobile targets such as ballistic-missile transporters. It will be able to operate autonomously in hostile airspace for extended periods and will incorporate the latest low-observable ('stealth') technology and enemy radar-jamming capabilities. The B-21 is part of a group of long-range strike systems that includes aircraft such as the B-1 and B-2 bombers, munitions, sensors, networks and electronic-warfare systems. It will have enhanced communications, processing power and networking capability with other aircraft and weapons. These systems can locate and hand off fleeting targets to the B-21. The bomber will also be equipped with a suite of sensors such as a multifunction, phased-array radar and self-protection systems able to deploy countermeasures against hostile aircraft.[6]

In summary, the full triad modernisation option as currently planned will provide redundant nuclear forces capable of inflicting unacceptable damage on the elements of national power valued by any potential adversaries including nuclear and conventional military forces, population, war-supporting industry, critical infrastructure, economic targets and political leadership. Table 5 provides a projected snapshot of US nuclear forces in 2035 based on current plans.

This force will have nearly 2,000 deliverable nuclear weapons, the great majority of which are many times more powerful than the nuclear weapons dropped on Japan (each of which were around 20 kilotons). It includes 850 warheads of 300 kilotons or more. The force will include three types of ballistic missiles with four types of warhead, one type of bomb and one type of cruise missile. At least 600 warheads will have 'selectable' yields of 0.3–150 kilotons that can be set for particular mission requirements.[7] This force will be capable

Table 5: **US nuclear forces, 2035 – full-triad option (current plan)**

Type	Designation	Number	Warheads × yield (kilotons)	Deployed warheads
ICBMs	GBSD	150	1 W87 × 300	150
	Minuteman III	250	1 W78 × 335	250
	Total	400		400
SLBMs[a]	UGM-133A *Trident* II (life extended)			
	Mk-4A	90	6 W76-1 × 100 (MIRV)	540
	Mk-5	90	5 W88 × 455 (MIRV)	450
	Total	180		990
Bombers	B-2[b]	20	5 LRSO/W80-4 × 5–150	100
			5 B61-12 × 0.3–50	100
	B-21[b]	40	5 LRSO/W80-4 × 5–150	200
			5 B61-12 × 0.3–50	200
	Total	60 (New START)	10 weapons per bomber as indicated above	600
	Total[c]			1,990 (actual) 1,450 (New START-accountable)

[a] Assumes five *Columbia* submarines with 16 missiles each and five *Ohio*-class with 20 missiles each.
[b] Assumes both B-2 and B-21 are equipped with five LRSO missiles and five B61-12 bombs, but they can carry more.
[c] This projected force structure would count as 1,450 'New START-accountable' warheads because each bomber is counted as one warhead under the treaty. This also assumes that the duration of the New START Treaty will be extended past 2035.

of penetrating or destroying any anticipated air- and missile-defence systems for decades.[8]

Three alternatives to the current plan

Option 1: Streamlined triad

The first of the three proposed alternatives to the existing plan is a 'streamlined triad'. This option would procure eight *Columbia*-class submarines instead of 12, and 300 replacement ICBMs instead of 400. The full fleet of 100 B-21 aircraft would be built as well as approximately 1,000 LRSO cruise missiles.

The streamlined triad includes production of the B61-12 and deployment of this weapon in the US and with NATO allies. The reduced number of SLBMs and ICBMs would mean that the streamlined triad force structure could support 1,100–1,550 operationally deployed and accountable warheads under New START counting rules and close to 2,000 actual warheads.

Like the full triad, the streamlined triad offers modernised nuclear forces that are rapidly employable in a crisis and could survive an initial attack and respond with devastating effect. This alternative would provide the US president with a diverse array of options for responding to the threat or use of nuclear weapons. These range from discriminate attacks on the military targets of the enemy that limit collateral damage, to counterforce attacks that would degrade an adversary's ability to damage the US, to massive attacks on urban areas and economic infrastructure.

In summary, the streamlined triad would provide redundant nuclear forces capable of inflicting unacceptable damage on the elements of national power valued by potential adversaries. Table 6 provides a projected snapshot of US nuclear forces in 2035 based on a streamlined triad.

Table 6: **US nuclear forces, 2035 – option 1: Streamlined triad**

Type	Designation	Number	Warheads × yield (kilotons)	Deployed warheads
ICBMs	GBSD	150	1 W87 × 300	150
	Minuteman III	150	1 W78 × 335	150
	Total	300		300
SLBMs[a]	UGM-133A *Trident* II (life extended)			
	Mk-4A	100	6 W76-1 × 100 (MIRV)	600
	Mk-5	80	6 W88 × 455 (MIRV)	480
	Total	180 (reduced to 128 by 2040)		1,080 (reduced to 768 by 2040)
Bombers	B-2[b]	20	5 LRSO/W80-4 × 5–150	100
			5 B61-12 × 0.3–50	100
	B-21[b]	40	5 LRSO/W80-4 × 5–150	200
			5 B61-12 × 0.3–50	200
	Total	60	Assumes 10 weapons per bomber as indicated above	600
	Total[c]			1,980 (actual)[d] 1,440 (New START-accountable)

[a] Assumes five *Columbia* submarines with 16 missiles each and five *Ohio*-class with 20 missiles each.
[b] Assumes both B-2 and B-21 can be equipped with five LRSO missiles and five B61-12 bombs.
[c] This projected force structure would count as 1,440 'New START-accountable' warheads because each bomber is counted as one warhead under the treaty. This also assumes that the duration of the New START Treaty has been extended past 2035.
[d] This number will fall as the SSBN force shrinks to eight *Columbia*-class submarines by 2040.

This alternative would give the US a nuclear force that in 2035 could deliver almost 2,000 nuclear weapons. This includes 780 warheads of 300 kilotons or more. The force would include three types of ballistic missiles, one type of bomb and one type of cruise missile. At least 600 warheads would have 'selectable' yields of 0.3–150 kilotons that could be set for particular mission requirements.[9] This force would be capable of penetrating or destroying any anticipated air- and missile-defence systems.

Option 2: Air–sea dyad

A second alternative to existing plans is to eliminate the ICBM leg of the nuclear force by 2030 and to rely on ten new *Columbia*-class submarines (rather than 12 as currently planned) and 80 B-21 strategic bombers (rather than 100), but without a nuclear cruise missile. Unless their elimination is required by a future arms-control treaty, some *Minuteman* III missiles and silos could be maintained for later use as satellite launchers or part of a conventional prompt global-strike system.

The air–sea dyad would involve production of the B61-12 guided nuclear bomb, but not its deployment with NATO allies. Rather, current variants of the B61 in Europe would be withdrawn to the US homeland as they reach the end of their service lives from 2021 and not replaced by new B61-12s deployed to NATO. Newly produced B61-12 bombs would be stored in reserve in the US. The decision to formally withdraw these weapons from NATO could be made in the context of a future treaty with Russia limiting tactical nuclear weapons.

If there was no agreement with Russia regarding tactical nuclear weapons, the US would find it politically more difficult to convince NATO to agree to remove the B61 bombs. NATO nuclear decisions are traditionally made by consensus. Eastern European and Baltic members of NATO in particular would likely oppose any withdrawal of US nuclear weapons from Europe if Russia made no reciprocal steps. However, even if removed, these weapons could be rapidly reintroduced if the need arose. In a conflict situation they could be delivered against the same targets by US strategic or tactical aircraft operating out of alternative US bases.

The slightly reduced number of SLBMs and the complete elimination of the *Minuteman* ICBM force mean that an air–sea dyad force structure could deploy 1,580 warheads in 2035 with diverse capabilities that could survive a first strike and deliver devastating retaliation. Under New START counting rules, however, the figure would be 1,040. This is because nuclear-bomber aircraft are counted as only one warhead under New START, whereas in practice under the terms of the treaty they can each carry up to 20 warheads. Under this option, as in option 1, bombers are assumed to carry ten nuclear weapons each. The nuclear LRSO and its W80-4 warhead would be cancelled, but long-range conventionally armed cruise missiles may be deployed on all strategic aircraft as well.

This second alternative proposes a triad of delivery vehicles until 2030 and then moves to a nuclear dyad of SSBNs and strategic bombers. A future force of ten new *Columbia*-class submarines would provide a reliable, flexible and survivable nuclear-weapons delivery system capable of launching hundreds of accurate, powerful nuclear warheads that can destroy civilian or military targets. Each *Columbia*-class submarine would carry 16 improved *Trident* II missiles, each able to carry up to eight nuclear warheads, although the analysis presented here assumes missiles are loaded with either five or six warheads per missile. Thus with ten new submarines (a level that would not be reached until the late-2030s), the SLBM leg of the dyad could carry 160 missiles with up to 960 warheads, with a capacity to upgrade to 1,280 warheads if required by changes in the strategic environment. With a fleet of ten SSBNs with reactors that run for the full lifetime of the hull, it is reasonable to assume that between six and eight submarines could be at sea continuously.

Under this alternative, there would be robust investment in the air-breathing leg intended to significantly enhance US capabilities to deliver nuclear and conventional weapons in both strategic and regional scenarios. It includes the planned procurement of 80 new B-21 strategic bombers with the initial aircraft estimated to begin service from 2025.

The air–sea dyad option would start retiring the *Minuteman* III missiles of the ICBM leg after 2030. If the *Minuteman* force was removed from the US triad unilaterally, there would be no restrictions on the type of warheads that some future configuration of land-based missiles could carry. Some stored *Minuteman* III missiles could be life-extended and equipped with hypersonic non-nuclear warheads with manoeuvring capability that could receive updated target information en route to targets. This means that they could be made more effective against mobile and relocatable targets in a future conflict. They might also be used to launch small satellites.

The retirement of the ICBM leg would have positive and negative consequences for deterrence. On the positive side, the smaller number of potential prompt-use warheads in the US arsenal would reduce concerns among potential adversaries that the US may attempt a disarming first strike on their forces and could thus improve strategic stability, lowering the chance of conflict. On the negative side, potential adversaries may believe that the elimination of the ICBM force leaves the US more vulnerable to a disarming first strike, because an adversary would only have to destroy US bombers and submarines. Yet these are the two most difficult legs of the US arsenal to target. Striking US air and submarine bases could kill many thousands of US civilians. Strikes on submarine bases would perhaps destroy some of the SSBNs, but at least four boats, with a minimum of 325 nuclear warheads, would be out on patrol and available to launch a devastating retaliatory strike.

Similarly, the US would have time to disperse its bomber force even in the event of a first strike by enemy ICBMs. Such action would likely be taken as a crisis mounted. US strategic aircraft can operate out of many more bases than their home bases in Missouri, North Dakota and Louisiana. William Perry, a former US secretary of defence, is certain that surviving forces would be sufficiently destructive to deter an enemy from launching a surprise attack:

> We have ample deterrence from the submarine force, and certainly if you add the bomber force to that, that's an overwhelming deterrence force. So I cannot understand the argument that we also need ICBMs for deterrence. We might need ICBMs for other reasons … but not for deterrence. Any sane nation would be deterred by the incredible striking power of our submarine force.[10]

In summary, the air–sea dyad option would provide redundant nuclear forces capable of inflicting unacceptable damage on the elements of national power valued by potential adversaries.

The air–sea dyad modernisation option would result in a force that in 2035 could deliver 1,580 warheads. This includes 480 warheads of 455 kilotons or more and 600 weapons with 'selectable' yields of 0.3–150 kilotons that can be set for particular mission requirements.[11] This force would include two types of ballistic-missile warheads and one type of bomb, with many hundreds of warheads in reserve and significant upload capa-

Table 7: **US nuclear forces, 2035 – option 2: Air–sea dyad**

Type	Designation	Number	Warheads × yield (kilotons)	Deployed warheads
ICBMs		0		0
SLBMs[a]	UGM-133A *Trident* II (life extended)			
	Mk-4A	100	5 W76-1 × 100 (MIRV)	500
	Mk-5	80	6 W88 × 455 (MIRV)	480
	Total	180		980
Bombers	B-2[b]	20	10 B61-12 × 0.3–50	200
	B-21[b]	40	10 B61-12 × 0.3–50	400
	Total	60		600
	Total[c]			1,580 (actual)[d] 1,040 (New START-accountable)

[a] Assumes five *Columbia* submarines with 16 missiles each and five *Ohio*-class with 20 missiles each.
[b] Assumes both B-2 and B-21 are equipped with ten B61-12 bombs, and that 60 bombers are nuclear-certified.
[c] This projected force structure would count as 1,040 New START-accountable warheads because each bomber is counted as one warhead under the treaty. This also assumes that the duration of the treaty has been extended past 2035.
[d] This number will fall as the SSBN force transitions to all *Columbia* submarines with 16 missiles each by 2040.

bility on SLBMs. This force would be capable of penetrating or destroying any anticipated air- and missile-defence systems and could deliver devastating retaliation even after absorbing a first strike. Table 7 provides a projected snapshot of US nuclear forces in 2035 based on an air–sea dyad.

Option 3: Dispersed maritime dyad
The third alternative reconfigures the dyad model to spread the sea-based deterrent across a larger number of submarines, namely six *Columbia*-class SSBNs and eight *Virginia*-class SSNs. As with the air–sea dyad, the ICBM leg would be eliminated around 2030. This force would include 80 new B-21 strategic aircraft without a nuclear-armed cruise missile and field 780 New START-accountable warheads and just over 1,266 actual, operationally deployed strategic warheads.

In common with the other proposed dyad, the dispersed maritime dyad foresees production of the B61-12 guided nuclear bomb, but not its deployment with NATO allies. Modernised

B61-12 bombs would be kept in storage in the US and current variants of the B61 in Europe would be withdrawn to the US as they reach the end of their service lives from 2021. Optimally, the decision to withdraw these weapons from NATO would be made in the context of a future treaty with Russia to limit tactical nuclear weapons.

Under this proposal, the first of six new *Columbia*-class SSBNs would enter the fleet in 2031 and would each be armed with 16 upgraded *Trident* II (D-5LE) SLBMs with six warheads each.

The dispersed maritime dyad would also innovatively add eight dual-purpose *Virginia*-class SSNs to the sea leg of the triad, each carrying four ballistic missiles in the Virginia Payload Module (VPM).[12] These missiles would carry an average of four warheads each. The *Virginia*-class SSNs combine the capabilities of an attack submarine – with conventional land attack, anti-ship and anti-submarine weapons systems – with the ability to deliver nuclear-armed SLBMs.

This configuration for the sea leg of the triad has several advantages. It places fewer nuclear warheads on a larger number of sea-based platforms, increasing the survivability of the at-sea deterrent. It also retains the undersea conventional land-attack capability that will be lost by 2025 with the retirement of four *Ohio*-class SSBNs that were converted to conventional cruise-missile carriers (SSGNs). In addition, it allows a larger portion of the platforms in the sea leg of the triad to contribute to conventional strategic missions, consistent with the concept of the 'New Triad' articulated in the 2002 and 2010 NPRs. This modernisation option allows at least eight nuclear ballistic-missile submarines to be on patrol at all times, taking the US closer to the patrol rates of the 1980s. It also delivers a numerically larger force of strategic nuclear-delivery vehicles than the other dyad at an equivalent cost, because the proven *Virginia*-class submarines are cheaper (at approximately US$2.7bn each) than *Columbia*-class submarines (estimated at US$4.5bn–5bn each). This option also mitigates a projected shortfall in US attack submarines in 2026–35.[13]

The plan for nuclear-warhead life-extension programmes under the dispersed maritime dyad are identical to the air–sea dyad. This includes cancellation of the W80-4 cruise missile warhead and interoperable warhead programme. The W78 and W87 ICBM warheads can be retired or placed in storage. The W88 and W76-1 SLBM warheads can undergo life extension as needed after 2030, and the need for a pit-manufacturing capability of 50–80 pits per year will be reduced.

The dispersed dyad provides a nuclear deterrent force that maintains a triad of delivery vehicles until 2030 and then moves to a nuclear dyad of SSBNs, SSNs and strategic bombers. This force structure can provide 1,266 deliverable nuclear warheads with diverse capabilities that can survive a first strike and deliver devastating retaliation.

The submarine force alone could provide a reliable, flexible and survivable nuclear-weapons delivery system capable of launching hundreds of accurate, powerful nuclear warheads that can destroy civilian or military targets. The *Trident* II missiles could be carried by both the *Columbia*- and *Virginia*-class submarines. Each of the six *Columbia* SSBNs would carry 16 missiles for a total of 96 missiles with six warheads each, giving a total of 576 warheads. The eight *Virginia*-class submarines would carry four SLBMs, each for a total of 32 missiles, armed with four warheads. Thus the combined future number of warheads on SLBMs would be 704 warheads on 128 SLBMs. These totals would not be reached until the *Columbia* and modified *Virginia* submarines were fully deployed from 2040. Until that time some *Ohio*-class SSBNs would remain in service with different missile loadings. Table 8 provides a snapshot of

Table 8: **US nuclear forces, 2035 – option 3: Dispersed maritime dyad**

Type	Designation	Number	Warheads × yield (kilotons)	Deployed
ICBMs		0		0
SLBMs[a]	UGM-133A *Trident* II (life extended)			
	Mk-4A	48	6 W76-1 × 100 (MIRV)	288
	Mk-5	60	6 W88 × 455 (MIRV)	360
	Modified *Trident* for VPM Mk-5	16	4 W88 × 455 (MIRV)	64
	Total	124		712
Bombers	B-2[b]	20	10 B61-12 × .0.3–50	200
	B-21[b]	40	10 B61-12 × 03–50	400
	Total	60		600
	Total[c]			1,312 (actual) 772 (New START-accountable)

[a] Assumes three *Columbia*-class submarines with 16 missiles; three *Ohio*-class with 20 missiles; and four *Virginia*-class with four missiles each.
[b] Assumes both B-2 and B-21 are equipped with ten B61-12 bombs, and that 60 bombers are nuclear-certified.
[c] This projected force structure would count as 772 New START-accountable warheads because each bomber is counted as one warhead under the treaty. This also assumes that the duration of the treaty has been extended past 2035.

Option 3 in 2035 as it is in transition to a dispersed maritime dyad.

As with the other dyad, the dispersed maritime dyad would feature 80 new strategic long-range strike bombers (B-21) estimated to enter service from 2025. As the new aircraft entered service, B-52 and B-1 bombers would be retired, although the plan calls for some of these aircraft to remain in service through the 2030s in non-nuclear roles. The 20 B-2 aircraft would be retained and upgraded.

This option would provide redundant nuclear forces capable of inflicting unacceptable damage on the elements of national power valued by potential adversaries.

As noted above the complete transition to a dispersed maritime dyad would result in a force that in the late 2030s or early 2040s could deliver 1,266 warheads, though under New START methodology the count would be 780. This includes 360 warheads of 455 kilotons and 600 weapons with 'selectable' yields of 0.3–150 kilotons that can be set for particular mission requirements.[14] This force would include two types of ballistic-missile warheads and one type of bomb, with many hundreds of warheads in reserve and significant upload capability on SLBMs. This force would be capable of penetrating or destroying any anticipated air- and missile-defence systems and delivering a devastating retaliation even after absorbing a first-strike. In addition, at least eight of the 14 ballistic-missile submarines can be kept at sea at all times, boosting the survivability of the sea leg of the dispersed dyad, as compared with the sea leg of the air–sea dyad.

CHAPTER THREE

Strategic stability and arms control

It is a long-standing US practice to ensure that the size and structure of the nuclear force, while maintaining deterrence, also supports and promotes strategic stability between the US and the other principal nuclear powers. This objective is reflected in current nuclear posture and employment guidance.

In the paradoxical world of nuclear strategy, efforts to achieve superiority over a rival can be self-defeating because they can induce destabilising actions by the rival, thereby reducing the security of both states. This is the classic security dilemma. It is particularly acute in the nuclear realm because changes in one state's nuclear arsenal, intended to make its forces more capable and its nuclear threats more credible to an adversary, can also stoke fears on the part of the adversary that it may be subject to a first strike designed to weaken its retaliatory potential. This lowers the nuclear threshold, with a potential adversary concluding it faces a 'use them or lose them' choice regarding its nuclear forces.

A fundamental lesson of nuclear strategy is therefore to see the balance of nuclear forces through the eyes of your potential nuclear-armed adversaries. In other words, in the nuclear age your adversaries' sense of security becomes your concern.[1] Nuclear-armed states must understand this consideration in order to avoid worsening the ever-present risk of nuclear conflict by miscalculation.

The prevention of miscalculation and distrust is facilitated by efforts to maintain a stable balance of nuclear forces between potential adversaries. Traditionally, strategic stability includes the absence of incentives by either side to use nuclear weapons first during a crisis (crisis stability), and the absence of incentives to rapidly or secretly build up their nuclear forces (arms-race stability).

Current US policy upholds the importance of maintaining strategic stability, as stated in the 2013 Report on Nuclear Employment Strategy:

> The United States seeks to maintain strategic stability with Russia. Consistent with the objective of maintaining an effective deterrent posture, the United States seeks to improve strategic stability by demonstrating that it is not our intent to negate Russia's strategic nuclear deterrent, or to destabilize the strategic military relationship with Russia.[2]

Strategic stability under the full triad

The current plans to modernise the full triad of US nuclear forces involve the acquisition of capabilities that exceed the requirements for deterrence, and may weaken both crisis and arms-race stability. Such an outcome would reduce US national security.

The most important nuclear relationship for the US is that with Russia, its sole peer in nuclear arms. Several aspects of existing US plans are alarming to Russian decision-makers and may create incentives for Russia to strike first in a future crisis, thus jeopardising crisis stability. Arms-race stability may also be imperilled, because aspects of the US programme might persuade Moscow that Washington intends to negate Russia's deterrent vis-à-vis the US, or at least to create such an imbalance in capability that the US will be more willing to threaten Russia's vital national interests (and if deterrence fails, to use its new weaponry in an early strike to vastly degrade Russia's ability to retaliate). If Russian assessments of US intentions shift in this direction, Russia will have a stronger incentive to accelerate its nuclear-weapons modernisation programmes, including some that the US and its allies regard as destabilising.

Three aspects of the current US plan to modernise its nuclear triad are particularly worrisome for Russia and, to some extent, China: an upgraded nuclear bomb, the B61-12 (see Figure 3); increased conventional- and nuclear-strike capabilities on new US strategic bombers, in particular the next-generation nuclear cruise missile; and improvements in the hard-target-kill capabilities of new US ICBMs and SLBMs.

The B61-12

Existing plans call for approximately 180 B61-12 bombs to be shared by Belgium, Germany, Italy, the Netherlands and Turkey from 2020 onwards. Another 220 or so will be stored on US territory. General Norton Schwartz, the former chief of staff of the US Air Force, confirmed the new military capabilities of the B61-12 in January 2014.[3] Compared with the current freefall or unguided nuclear bombs deployed in Europe, the B61-12 will be guided by a new tail kit assembly enabling it to strike targets more accurately with a smaller explosive yield and less radioactive fallout. The net result is that the B61-12 is more likely to be used in a conflict situation crossing the threshold from conventional to nuclear war. If set at its more powerful explosive yield, this accuracy also means the B61-12 will be effective against hardened or underground targets such as military command centres or aircraft shelters.

Figure 3: **The B61-12 nuclear bomb**

Photo: Randy Montoya/Sandia National Laboratories

In September 2015 the Russian foreign ministry expressed its opposition to the planned NATO deployment of the B61-12 on a new generation of stealth aircraft including the US F-35 *Lightning* II.[4] Such aircraft, if forward-deployed to NATO bases in Estonia, Lithuania, Poland and Romania during a crisis, could reach Russia's largest cities in 15–20 minutes – not much longer than the flight time of the *Pershing* II ballistic missiles eliminated by the 1987 INF Treaty. In response to planned B61-12 deployments, Russia has threatened to deploy nuclear-armed *Iskander* tactical missiles to Kaliningrad, its exclave on the Baltic coast between Lithuania and Poland. Temporary deployments of this missile system took place in October 2016 for the purposes of exercises.

The *Iskander*-M has a range of 400km, can carry several varieties of 700kg warhead, including nuclear, and is accurate to within five metres. The *Iskander* has the capability to retarget in flight, enabling it to engage mobile targets including ships. The positioning of nuclear warheads for the *Iskander* in Kaliningrad could threaten an array of military and political targets across European NATO states.[5] The weapons would take only a few minutes to reach several NATO capitals. As shown in Figure 4, Russia already bases some tactical nuclear weapons on its border with the Baltics and Eastern Ukraine. If forward-deployed, those nuclear weapons would increase Russia–NATO tensions, weaken nuclear stability in Europe and increase pressure on NATO to destroy these weapons first if a conventional conflict broke out. These are precisely the outcomes that US nuclear strategy seeks to avoid.

The LRSO

The US government's default plan also calls for the development and deployment of the LRSO nuclear-armed cruise

Figure 4: **Locations of US and Russian tactical nuclear weapons in Europe**

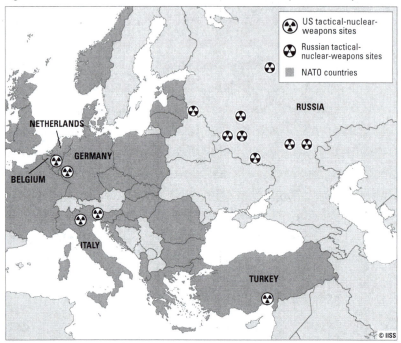

Republished with permission of *Foreign Affairs*, from Barry Blechman and Russell Rumbaugh, 'Bombs Away: The Case for Phasing Out U.S. Tactical Nukes in Europe', *Foreign Affairs*, vol. 93, no. 4, July–August 2014; permission conveyed through Copyright Clearance Center, Inc.

missile on B-52H and B-2 bombers and the new B-21 aircraft from 2025 onwards; the LRSO will replace the current nuclear-armed ALCM. The US Air Force has not disclosed the specific capabilities of the LRSO. According to media reports, the new missile is likely to be faster, stealthier and more accurate, and have longer range and manoeuvring capability than the ALCM. Its nuclear warhead will have improved variable yield and the missile may be retargetable in flight.[6]

Deployment of the LRSO could weaken stability and signal to Russia that the US believes nuclear weapons retain signifi-cant war-fighting value. Other US nuclear-weapons systems already cover the target set that the LRSO is intended to engage. Strategic and tactical aircraft, ICBMs and SLBMs can strike such targets if the nuclear threshold has been crossed.

If hostilities remain conventional, the US possesses a rapidly expanding capability to strike targets with existing and planned conventional cruise missiles launched from multiple aircraft types. In fact, the US Air Force is fielding thousands of new conventional cruise missiles that provide all the stand-off capability needed to keep bombers out of harm's way, degrade enemy air defences, and destroy fixed and mobile soft, medium and even some hard targets with high accuracy – the same missions for which defence officials say the LRSO is needed.

These conventional cruise missiles are the Joint Air-to-Surface Standoff Missile (JASSM) and its extended-range version (JASSM–ER). Plans call for the acquisition of more than 5,000 JASSMs and at least 2,978 JASSM–ERs. Full-scale production of the JASSM–ER was authorised in 2014 and the weapon is already deployed on B-1 bombers, each of which can carry 24 missiles. The JASSM–ER will be integrated on most US strategic and tactical aircraft – including the B-52H, B-1, B-2, B-21, F-15, F-16, F-18 and F-35 – during the next decade. Aircraft can employ the JASSM–ER against high-value or highly defended targets from outside the lethal range of air defences (up to 925km).[7]

Acquisition of a nuclear-armed LRSO in addition to the JASSM system implies that the US strategy includes options for tactical nuclear strikes early in a conflict intended to respond to nuclear use, signal resolve or destroy as much of an adversary's nuclear retaliatory potential as possible. Maintaining concepts and capabilities for nuclear employment for tactical war-fighting purposes that could be accomplished just as effectively by conventional weapons is contrary to guidance contained in the 2010 NPR and the 2013 Report on Nuclear Employment Strategy, which supports establishing deterrence with the fewest nuclear weapons possible.

Thus the LRSO potentially undermines crisis stability and threatens arms-race stability. Acquisition of the LRSO increases the likelihood of reciprocal developments by Russia. Moscow has deployed a small number of new ground-launched cruise missiles (GLCM) that could carry a nuclear or conventional warhead and have a range greater than 500km. This system (named the SSC-X-8 by NATO, or R-500 *Iskander*-K in some US media reports) has been tested on the *Iskander* mobile launcher. The US Department of State alleges that the new missile violates the INF Treaty,[8] which banned all US and Soviet ground-launched ballistic and cruise missiles with ranges of 500–5,500km.

The treaty entered into force in June 1988. Within three years, the two countries had destroyed around 2,600 missiles – the first time that an entire class of nuclear arms had been eliminated. The most significant achievement of the treaty was to eliminate nuclear weapons that, because of their short flight times, made early warning problematic and reduced the time in which leaders must decide the fate of millions of citizens. These conditions undermine stability and raise the risk of pre-emptive attacks or mistakes.[9] A return to such a dangerous stand-off in Europe is not in the security interests of NATO. However, this outcome becomes more likely with the planned US deployment of B61-12 nuclear bombs on NATO aircraft and LRSO nuclear cruise missiles, and possible additional Russian deployments of new ground-launched nuclear cruise missiles and tactical, nuclear-armed *Iskander* ballistic missiles.

Hard-target-kill warheads and the 'new triad'

A third aspect of the default US plan that has the potential to undermine strategic stability with Russia and China is the development of increasingly accurate, hard-target-kill ballistic-missile warheads, in combination with advances in conventional weapons that can be used to destroy enemy nuclear forces, and improving ballistic-missile defences. This conception of US strategic forces, called the 'New Triad', was first described in the 2002 NPR.[10] US conventional long-range strike capabilities, and missile-defence capabilities, have now been deployed in sufficient numbers to influence the strategic nuclear calculus of potential adversaries. Any current description of strategic stability must take these forces into account.

According to defence analyst James Acton, Russia and China have voiced concerns that the growing inventory of US long-range, high-precision conventional weapons, including cruise missiles as well as developmental weapons such as 'boost-glide' systems, could be used to attack their nuclear forces before launch, while ballistic-missile defences could 'mop up' any that survived and were launched. These fears – whether or not they are technically justified – could lead to anxieties about the possibility of a pre-emptive strike during a crisis and thus undermine stability.[11] As a 2013 RAND study noted: 'During an international crisis, posturing powerful strike forces in a way that suggests that a surprise attack is imminent can lead an opponent to conclude that it has no alternative but to launch a preemptive strike.'[12]

Russian President Vladimir Putin said in December 2013 that, in combination with ballistic-missile defence, conventional prompt global strike weapons 'could negate all previous agreements on the limitation and reduction of strategic nuclear weapons, and disrupt the strategic balance of power'.[13] A weapons-system concept that could be particularly destabilising is the hypersonic boost-glide vehicle. These weapons would be launched into the outer reaches of Earth's atmosphere by ballistic missiles and then glide down to their targets at supersonic speeds. The speed of re-entry into the atmosphere would generate destructive energy exceeding that of a similar mass of conventional high explosives, thus potentially allowing them to destroy hard military targets.

The trend towards conventionally armed global-strike weapons is not limited to the US. Both Russia and China are developing such weapons, although these are less advanced. None of the three states has yet completed testing or deployment of boost-glide vehicles.

The US leads the world in the deployment of modern ballistic-missile defences. In 2001, then-president George W. Bush authorised the deployment of the Ground-Based Midcourse Defense (GMD) system to protect the US homeland against small numbers of ballistic missiles launched from North Korea or Iran. The effectiveness of this system has been called into question, and it does not have the capability to negate the threat posed by Russian or Chinese long-range nuclear-armed ballistic missiles.[14] The GMD interceptor successfully engaged a target with the velocity of an ICBM warhead for the first time in May 2017.[15] However, it has not been tested successfully against ICBMs with sophisticated decoys and other countermeasures, which would complicate the interception of a real enemy warhead.

Greater success has been achieved with the shorter-range missile interceptors that have been deployed for the defence of European and Asian allies. For example, the system of sea- and land-based missile defences for Europe known as the European Phased Adaptive Approach (EPAA) has entered its third phase of deployment, which is due to be completed in 2018. By that time, EPAA interceptors will be operational from bases in Deveselu, Romania, and Redzikowo, Poland, and from more than 30 surface ships that can be based in the Mediterranean, North, Barents or Black Seas. Even this system will have very little capability against Russian ICBMs and SLBMs, but Russia has consistently complained that it is designed to undermine the strategic nuclear balance.[16]

Russia and China view the United States' plans to modernise its nuclear triad in the context of emerging US non-nuclear strategic offensive weapons and improving missile defences described above. It is the integration of advanced conventional, missile-defence and nuclear weaponry that most concerns them. US ICBM and SLBM warheads have become increasingly effective counterforce weapons in the last 10–15 years and are set to become even more so, before the first new *Columbia* SSBN or GBSD replacement missile enters service.

For example, a multibillion-dollar, decade-long modernisation programme to extend the service life of the current *Minuteman* III ICBM to 2030 has been completed. The upgraded *Minuteman* IIIs are basically new missiles except for the shell. Part of the upgrade involved improving the accuracy and capability of the warheads to destroy hard targets. The Air Force is also upgrading the *Minuteman*'s nuclear warheads by partially replacing older W78 warheads with newer and more powerful W87 warheads, which were formerly deployed on the now-retired MX *Peacekeeper* ICBMs. Under a 2004 LEP, the W87 warhead was refurbished to extend its service life past 2025.[17]

With respect to SLBMs, starting in 2017 the *Trident* II life-extended (LE) missile will be back-fitted onto existing *Ohio*-class submarines for the remainder of their service lives (up to 2042), and will have a new guidance system designed to provide flexibility to support new missions and make the missile more accurate. The *Trident* II–LE will also be deployed on the first *Columbia*-class submarines from 2031. These upgraded SLBMs will carry either the newly refurbished W76-1 or the more powerful W88 warheads.

As shown in Table 5, these upgrades will offer US war planners 990 hard-target-kill SLBM warheads that are constantly available, even with two submarines in overhaul. The US has reportedly deployed a new fuse on its SLBMs, giving this leg of the triad alone more than three times the number of warheads needed to destroy the entire fleet of Russian land-based missiles in their silos.[18] It is this capability, combined with conventional global-strike weapons and improving missile defences, that affects strategic stability and creates incentives for Russian and Chinese strategic-modernisation programmes. They also provide justification for Russia and potentially China to maintain and exercise the ability to launch their nuclear forces under warning of attack from the US, to avoid losing their nuclear forces to a devastating first strike.

In fact, some observers assert that Russia, fearing a surprise attack from US conventional and nuclear weapons, has already shortened its time to launch on warning, and pre-authorised military commanders to launch retaliatory strikes. Reportedly, top military command posts in the Moscow area can now bypass the entire human chain of command and directly fire, by remote control, rockets in silos and on trucks as far away as Siberia in only 20 seconds.[19] This development, if true, is not in the national-security interests of the US or its NATO allies.

Recent analysis indicates that China is considering a major change to its nuclear posture in response to the emerging new triad. This change would, for the first time, put a portion of China's ICBM force on alert so that the missiles could be launched rapidly in a crisis or in retaliation to warning of an attack.[20] Such a move by China could undermine stability in a crisis by increasing the risk of an accidental, unauthorised or mistaken nuclear launch. China currently keeps its nuclear weapons off alert, with nuclear warheads not mated to the delivery vehicles. This makes an unauthorised or accidental launch of an armed ballistic missile towards the US a remote possibility. Yet US plans to replicate its nuclear triad in full, with upgraded capabilities, might well provide China with the motivation to change its posture, given the context of improvements in missile defence and conventional strategic weapons. This would weaken the security of the US and its allies.

Both Russia and China are developing new heavy ICBMs with multiple independently targetable re-entry vehicles (MIRVs) that can carry ten or more nuclear warheads each. This trend runs counter to previous efforts by the US and Russia to move to single-warhead ICBMs in order to strengthen strategic stability. Reducing the number of warheads on each ICBM improves stability by preventing one missile from threatening multiple targets in a first strike and reducing incentives to destroy MIRV missiles before they are launched.

The Russian missile is the SS-X-30 *Sarmat* (or *Satan* II). It is liquid-fuelled and silo-based and would replace the SS-18 *Satan* heavy ICBM. It can carry 10–15 warheads and multiple decoys and countermeasures to evade missile defences. It may also be capable of delivering hypersonic glide vehicles. *Sarmat* is expected to enter active service in 2018, with all 50 missiles currently on order fielded by 2020.[21]

The Chinese missile is the DF-41. US intelligence agencies estimate that it can carry up to ten 150–300-kiloton thermonuclear warheads and is capable of targeting the entire continental US. It is solid-fuelled, road-mobile and possibly also intended to be rail-based, similar to the former Soviet SS-24 rail-based ICBM. The missile is designed to carry multiple countermeasures to overcome missile-defence systems. It will likely be deployed in unknown quantities starting at some point in 2018–20.[22]

These Russian and Chinese systems are still in development, so there is a chance that they could be delayed, reduced or deployed with fewer warheads than currently estimated. However, the prospects for this are slim if the US proceeds with its plans for modernisation of the full triad of its nuclear forces.

Strategic stability under the alternatives

The first alternative plan, for a streamlined triad, is almost as damaging to strategic stability as the US government's default plan. It would endow the US with nuclear capabilities that exceed the requirements for deterrence, potentially signalling that it intends to undermine Russia's deterrent and to seek strategic primacy. Like the current modernisation plan, this option may weaken both crisis stability and arms-race stability. Even though the number of US ICBMs and SLBMs would be reduced, it would be straightforward to add more warheads and arrive at a deployed strategic nuclear arsenal close to currently planned New START levels. Moreover, the proposed streamlined force would retain more than 1,300 actual missile warheads, 600 bomber weapons and more than 1,000 hard-target-kill warheads at all times.

The streamlined triad option therefore remains somewhat destabilising because it includes the three characteristics of the default plan that are most worrying to Moscow: the B61-12 guided bomb, to be deployed in Europe; the LRSO cruise missile; and improved strategic warheads with enhanced capabilities to destroy hard targets.

The air–sea dyad and the dispersed maritime dyad, by contrast, would send a strong signal that the US intended to reduce the role of nuclear weapons in its strategy and aspired to achieve deterrence with fewer such weapons. Cancelling the planned nuclear LRSO cruise missile and keeping the B61-12 bomb out of Europe distances the US from the concept of nuclear employment for tactical war-fighting and keeps the nuclear threshold as high as possible. Ideally, a US offer to cancel the LRSO could lead to an arms-control agreement with Russia to ban all nuclear-armed cruise missiles sometime before 2020.[23]

By shifting to a dyad force structure, the US would greatly reassure Russia that it did not intend to negate Russia's deterrent by launching a successful counterforce first strike based on strategic primacy – in other words, it acknowledges mutual strategic vulnerability. Retirement of the *Minuteman* III ICBM force would largely obviate Russian concerns that its own land-based missile force, both silo and mobile ICBMs, which carries most of its nuclear warheads, could be destroyed in a surprise US attack. Without the 400 powerful warheads on the *Minuteman* III missiles, the US would have less confidence that it could attack Russia's strategic forces and retain enough reserve weapons to deter or defeat a Russian retaliation with its surviving forces. Once *Minuteman* III was retired, Russia would have 400 fewer targets to hit if it contemplated a first strike against the US. It might therefore allocate more missiles to strike the US submarine force. However, Russia would still face the daunting fact that at least five US SSBNs would survive any attack and launch a devastating retaliation. In fact, retirement of the US ICBM leg of the triad would largely negate the investment that Russia has devoted to modernisation of its ICBM force in the past 20 years, because it would leave this force without logical targets while at the same time doing little or nothing to reduce strategic stability.[24]

Arms control and nuclear modernisation

Arms control has long been an element of US nuclear strategy. It can contribute to international stability by limiting the development, production, stockpiling and deployment of weapons. Arms-control regimes also codify and enforce these mutually agreed-upon force levels and structures, fostering understanding, support for the rule of law, cooperation and even trust. This can help shift a relationship from one based upon unpredictable, coercive formulations of deterrence by punishment to one characterised by mutual restraint.[25]

This is why the US has engaged bilaterally with the Soviet Union and then Russia for nearly 50 years to reach agreements that control or reduce nuclear arsenals. It is why the US and its allies have supported dozens of multilateral legal instruments to control or reduce weapons of mass destruction and prevent their spread to additional states or non-state actors. Any US nuclear-weapons modernisation plans should consider how those new systems can strengthen existing arms-control agreements and preserve opportunities for new agreements.

The full and streamlined triad plans could both undermine the New START Treaty because of their implications for strategic stability with Russia. New START limits on strategic forces expire in 2021 unless the US and Russia agree to extend the treaty to 2026. By 2028, full triad plans call for the B-21 bomber, the B61-12 guided nuclear bomb and the LRSO to be in full-scale deployment. More-effective US missile-defence systems will also be installed in Romania and Poland and upgraded interceptor missiles deployed aboard Navy vessels.[26] As outlined above, Russia will find some of these deployments destabilising, particularly the B61-12 with NATO forces, the LRSO and improved missile defences. It might therefore determine that the New START limits no longer suit its strategic interests, in particular the level of forces it needs to sustain deterrence vis-à-vis the US. In that instance Russia would let the treaty expire. It might also accelerate deployments of intermediate-range nuclear forces such as the SSC-X-8 and the *Iskander* and withdraw from the INF Treaty.[27] Either of these outcomes would be contrary to US strategic objectives.

The streamlined triad modernisation option could also cause Russia to rely more on mobile, forward-deployed non-strategic nuclear forces, or China to increase the alert level of its nuclear missiles. As discussed in Chapter 4, the further global spread of nuclear weapons, even to new locations within countries that already possess them, can raise the risk of terrorists stealing or sabotaging them, and increases the chance of them being used in conflict.

With regard to support for current and future nuclear-arms-control efforts, the full and streamlined triad options do little to address potential threats to strategic stability or create options for innovative arms-control proposals. The decisions to transfer upgraded nuclear bombs with improved performance capabilities to NATO countries and to produce an improved, stealthy, long-range nuclear cruise missile do not lend themselves to resolving issues with the INF Treaty or seeking a pullback of nuclear forces from the European theatre. Instead, they potentially raise tensions and imply a willingness to return to a Cold War-style nuclear stand-off between NATO and Russia.

An alternative course of action, which is consistent with the two dyad options, would be to explore with Russia new arms-control proposals that could result in pulling back all US nuclear weapons from the territory of NATO allies and banning nuclear-armed cruise missiles. In the case of the LRSO, development of a conventionally armed air-launched cruise missile could go ahead if required, but the W80-4 warhead could be delayed and only developed if Russia refused to negotiate a new, cooperative nuclear agreement with NATO that de-emphasised the role of nuclear weapons and reaffirmed mutual compliance with the INF Treaty.

The two dyad options offer unique opportunities for further negotiated reductions in both strategic and tactical delivery vehicles and warheads. Russia has recently stated that it remains interested in further arms reductions if they include NATO nuclear forces.[28] Both dyad options call for the eventual removal of NATO nuclear weapons from Belgium, Germany, the Netherlands, Italy and Turkey. If NATO indicated a willingness to adopt these plans, Russia might be prepared to cancel its new nuclear GLCM, pull its tactical nuclear weapons back from European borders, and pledge never to deploy nuclear weapons in front-line territories such as Crimea or Kaliningrad.

Similarly, announcing willingness to retire the ICBM leg of the US triad by 2030 would reduce incentives for Russia to complete development and deployment of the ten-warhead *Sarmat* ICBM. Mutual restraint in ICBM modernisation could create an opportunity to negotiate a new round of reductions to strategic delivery vehicles and deployed warheads. One objective of such negotiations could be to formalise limits of approximately 1,000 New START-accountable warheads on 600 strategic delivery vehicles. Another could be to revive the requirement under the never-ratified START II Treaty that ICBMs be limited to a single warhead.[29]

Future-proofing

Assuming that the goals of nuclear non-proliferation – reducing the threat of nuclear terrorism, and the eventual elimination of nuclear weapons – remain key objectives of US and allied national-security strategy, there is value in procuring nuclear systems that could be switched to non-nuclear purposes in the future.

The 'designing for denuclearisation' philosophy has broad implications for procurement decisions across the full range of nuclear-weapons infrastructure, including nuclear-warhead production and dismantlement facilities, strategic nuclear-delivery platforms, arms-control and verification technology, and dual-purpose systems such as aircraft and cruise missiles.[30] Designing for denuclearisation would seek modernisation strategies that created opportunities for verifying negotiated nuclear arms-control or reciprocal agreements that further reduced nuclear arsenals.

This approach would build in certain features and capabilities to expensive, long-service-life facilities and weapons platforms that would benefit a national-security strategy favouring a reduced role for nuclear weapons. The actual use of these capabilities would depend on the evolution of the security environment and increased efforts at collective security, but would also signal a desire on the part of the US and its allies to lead and shape that evolution. In essence, designing for denuclearisation would be similar to a hedge strategy because it would seek to provide US nuclear-weapons infrastructure and operational forces with characteristics that could facilitate verified arms-control agreements, increase transparency, improve strategic stability and simplify conversion to non-nuclear missions.

A like-for-like replacement of the Cold War nuclear triad as envisioned by the existing US modernisation plan may actually undercut some of these objectives. The dyad options, conversely, can be aligned with designing for denuclearisation. For example, the removal of ICBMs from silos could be verified easily using satellite or other airborne imagery, and under the dispersed maritime dyad the nuclear missiles could be easily removed from *Virginia*-class SSNs and the boats would require only minor modification to be certified as conventional-only platforms. In addition, if the security environment improved, completing the construction of *Virginia*-class boats as non-nuclear-weapon platforms would be less costly. For nuclear-only platforms, it would be much more difficult to take advantage of the sunk costs. New *Columbia*-class SSBNs would have to be redesigned or extensively converted to non-nuclear missions, as was the case with the four *Ohio*-class SSBNs that were converted into SSGNs.[31]

CHAPTER FOUR

Nuclear security and non-proliferation

Decisions concerning the renewal of the nuclear arsenal also bear directly on the US objective to support nuclear non-proliferation globally, including through international agreements. US security depends on preventing the proliferation of nuclear weapons, which is near-universally regarded as increasing the risk of a conflict involving nuclear weapons – or of those weapons falling into the wrong hands. US nuclear weapons and materials must be secure from the threat of efforts by state or non-state actors to steal or sabotage them. The goals of nuclear security and non-proliferation are articulated in all official documents on US nuclear strategy.

Nuclear security

The 2013 Report on Nuclear Employment Strategy stated 'Today's most immediate and extreme danger remains nuclear terrorism.'[1] This danger persists and was recently highlighted by the Defense Science Board's 'Seven Priorities for the New Administration' report, and Harvard University's Belfer Center for Science and International Affairs.[2] The crux of this threat is the real possibility that terrorists or non-state actors could acquire fissile material or nuclear weapons, and the certainty that they would have the motivation to use them against the US or its allies. This motivation is not tempered by the threat of nuclear retaliation, as is the case in state-to-state deterrence. The social, political and economic consequences of the detonation of even a crude terrorist nuclear bomb in any major urban area would be severe, so any plan to modernise nuclear forces should take this risk into account.

No country can achieve perfect security for its nuclear forces and facilities. The choice that the US makes regarding the future structure of its nuclear arsenal affects nuclear security, because the options differ in terms of the opportunities they present to a would-be nuclear terrorist. For example, modernisation choices that increase the routine ground transportation of nuclear weapons or their components outside protected bases could increase the risk of nuclear terrorism, because these items are more vulnerable to attack when they are on public roads and railways or left in exposed locations. The vulnerability of nuclear weapons that are dispersed at isolated bases must also be considered, as well as the vulnerability of all weapons to cyber sabotage.

Another consideration is what impact US modernisation plans will have on other nuclear states' posture and operational deployments. If any nuclear states react to US modernisation by increasing deployments of tactical nuclear weapons into remote areas where they could be vulnerable to attack, this in turn could increase the chance of nuclear terrorism against the US or its allies. A weapon stolen anywhere could be used against NATO states or US bases abroad.

Furthermore, in the context of reducing the threat of nuclear terrorism, the trade-offs that must be made between spending on nuclear modernisation and other national-security capabilities are particularly relevant. Nuclear-security programmes such as counter-nuclear-smuggling efforts, nuclear-material detection, nuclear-weapons protection and accounting, nuclear search teams, emergency response and foreign aid for nuclear security are intended to directly reduce the nuclear terrorist threat.

If funding for these programmes is reduced because comprehensive nuclear modernisation has been given higher priority, the nuclear-terrorism threat may not be combatted adequately. The president's FY2017 budget, supporting the full triad modernisation option, continues a potentially dangerous trend that started in 2014.[3] For example, funds for the DoE's global nuclear-material security programme were reduced from US$426.8m in FY2016 to US$337.1m in FY2017.[4] President Donald Trump's first budget calls for even deeper reductions to nuclear-security programmes while requesting sharp increases for nuclear-weapons and warhead modernisation. The Trump administration's five-year budget request for new nuclear weapons is roughly US$570bn more than projected in FY2017; the proposal for core nuclear-terrorism prevention and non-proliferation programmes is more than US$200m less than projected. Moreover, the budget request for security for US nuclear weapons showed a modest US$4m increase, from US$682m to US$686m between FY2016 and FY2018, which is probably a slight decrease taking inflation into account.[5]

The full triad exceeds anticipated defence budgets for 10–20 years, therefore constraining funding available for programmes to counter nuclear smuggling, detect nuclear materials, and protect and account for nuclear weapons. It also restricts funding for: nuclear search teams that would be the first responders to a nuclear terrorist incident and would try to recover stolen nuclear weapons or materials before they could be detonated; emergency response capabilities; and foreign aid for nuclear security to states such as NATO allies, Russia,

Figure 5: **Requested and allocated funding for US Department of Energy nuclear-security programmes, 2009–17**

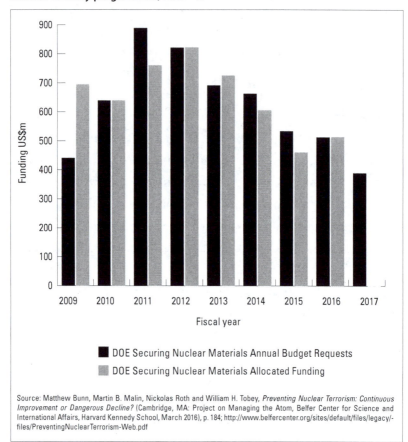

Source: Matthew Bunn, Martin B. Malin, Nickolas Roth and William H. Tobey, *Preventing Nuclear Terrorism: Continuous Improvement or Dangerous Decline?* (Cambridge, MA: Project on Managing the Atom, Belfer Center for Science and International Affairs, Harvard Kennedy School, March 2016), p. 184; http://www.belfercenter.org/sites/default/files/legacy/-files/PreventingNuclearTerrorism-Web.pdf

Pakistan and many others that have small quantities of weapons-usable fissile materials. The current trend of underfunding these activities, as illustrated in Figure 5, increases the risk of nuclear terrorism.

Nuclear security under the triad and dyad plans

The US government's current plan for nuclear modernisation does very little to reduce the risk of nuclear terrorism. The full triad represents the largest deployed force of nuclear warheads and delivery vehicles of all four options considered in this study, and therefore has the disadvantage of requiring the largest number of locations for these assets and the greatest number of ongoing nuclear-weapon shipments and maintenance activities. The greater the number of nuclear-weapon deployment sites and shipments, the greater the opportunities for theft or sabotage.

One of the most troubling aspects of the default plan, from the perspective of nuclear security, concerns the modernised B61-12 bomb to be deployed with US allies in Europe. A US DoD task force has raised concerns about the security of US nuclear weapons in Europe.[6] Similar concerns and changes in the regional security environment led to the withdrawal of US nuclear weapons from Greece in 2001, one of two bases in Germany in 2005 and the UK in 2006.

In 2008 an internal US Air Force investigation determined that 'most sites' currently used for deploying nuclear weapons in Europe did not meet DoD security requirements.[7] In 2010 a group of activists managed to penetrate Kleine Brogel Air Base in Belgium, where the US Air Force currently deploys 10–20 nuclear bombs.[8] The US is in the process of upgrading security at its two largest overseas nuclear-weapons bases, Incirlik in Turkey and Aviano in Italy, acknowledging that protection from terrorism or state-backed saboteurs at the bases is no longer adequate to meet a growing threat. Upgrades are also planned for bases in Belgium, Germany and the Netherlands.[9]

Since 2015 there have been numerous terrorist attacks in Turkey, along with a failed military coup in 2016. States in Western Europe including Belgium, France and the UK have also been the targets of terrorist attacks. Although civilians were the principal target of attacks in Europe, there is no guarantee that military bases will not be targeted in future. Moreover, at the time of writing there is little basis for assuming that the terrorist threat is receding in Europe or Turkey:

terror attacks were occurring with increasing frequency in the UK and Germany in the spring and summer of 2017. This trend may continue and intensify.

The ICBM force in the full and streamlined triads is perhaps the element of the US nuclear arsenal most vulnerable to a cyber attack. Such an attack could sabotage the system, cause a serious accident, initiate an unauthorised launch, or appear to be an attack from a potential adversary such as Russia or China in order to catalyse a conflict. At a Senate Armed Services Committee hearing in March 2013, General C. Robert Kehler, then head of US Strategic Command (STRATCOM), said he was 'very concerned with the potential of a cyber-related attack on our nuclear command and control and on the weapons systems themselves'.[10]

Another potential trade-off that affects the chances of nuclear terrorism is between the nuclear weapons themselves and the security forces and equipment that protect them. For example, in addition to protecting nuclear-weapon transportation convoys, US ICBM security forces also have an 'alert mission requirement' to respond to an attack on any of the silos or launch facilities. These forces currently operate Vietnam-era UH-1 (*Huey*) helicopters with limited speed, distance and payload capabilities. In February 2016, then-STRATCOM commander Cecil Haney confirmed that the UH-1N helicopters do not fully meet current ICBM complex security requirements as outlined by the DoD and STRATCOM.[11] As of October 2016, the Air Force had not committed funding to purchase a new fleet of helicopters until 2019 because of other aircraft acquisition priorities.[12]

The streamlined triad includes 300 ICBMs, rather than the 400 under the default modernisation plan. The smaller missile force would be somewhat easier to protect from physical attack, but not cyber intrusion. Moreover, deployment of the B61-12 nuclear bombs to NATO states also means that the streamlined triad would not reduce the number of areas to which US nuclear weapons are deployed. Given the rapidly evolving conflicts on NATO's borders, and increased terror activity in Belgium, Germany and Turkey, guaranteeing the security of nuclear weapons deployed with NATO will become increasingly difficult.[13] If security at NATO nuclear storage sites has not been or cannot be improved quickly and adequately, consideration should be given to pulling all remaining US nuclear weapons from Europe as an urgent measure to improve NATO security and reduce the chances of nuclear terrorism.

Like the full triad, the streamlined triad would exceed anticipated defence budgets for 10–20 years, and therefore would also consume resources that alternatively could go towards counter-nuclear-smuggling efforts, nuclear-material detection, nuclear-weapons protection and accounting, nuclear search teams, emergency response, and foreign aid for nuclear security. These programmes are intended to directly reduce the nuclear-terrorist threat. If a streamlined triad modernisation option was given higher priority, less funding would be available for these programmes, and the nuclear-terrorism threat may not be adequately tackled.

The two dyad options are preferable for several reasons with respect to reducing the risk of nuclear terrorism, offering several advantages over the triads. Firstly, they would reduce the number of locations for US and NATO nuclear weapons, thus reducing the number of facilities that need protecting from actors seeking to acquire or sabotage a nuclear weapon. They would also eliminate the need to transport nuclear weapons to and within Europe, in locations where security requirements are becoming harder to meet. Secondly, they would reduce incentives for Russia and China to forward-deploy non-strategic nuclear weapons or place more weapons on alert or in a launch-on-warning posture where they could be more vulnerable to cyber attack. Cancellation of the LRSO might boost the chances of negotiating a ban on nuclear-armed cruise missiles, many of which would be forward-deployed and so potentially an attractive target for theft or sabotage. Thirdly, they both cost at least US$400bn less over 30 years than the full triad, almost a 45% reduction in the estimated cost of modernising the US nuclear arsenal.[14] The funds made available by these savings could be shifted to programmes that directly address the nuclear-terrorism threat. As noted above, funding for those programmes has been cut by one-third in 2011–16, while funding for the modernisation of nuclear forces has increased during the same period.[15] Retirement of the ICBM leg would increase nuclear security because those missiles have a troubling track record with regard to equipment security and human performance.

The most direct and effective way that dyad modernisation plans could tackle the risks of nuclear terrorism is by freeing up major financial resources within the defence budget that could be applied to the nuclear-counter-terrorism mission. The air–sea dyad option would save an estimated US$432bn, and the dispersed maritime dyad US$443bn over 30 years compared to the default plan. Some of the saved resources could be used to expand programmes that counter nuclear-smuggling efforts, nuclear-material detection, nuclear-weapons protection and accounting, nuclear search teams, emergency response and foreign aid for nuclear security. All of these directly reduce the nuclear terrorist threat.[16]

In addition, the removal of the ICBM leg eliminates the risk, noted by the STRATCOM commander, of a cyber attack on the most automated, prompt-use nuclear-weapons system. The results of such an attack could range from systems malfunctioning, to an accident, to an unauthorised launch that could trigger a nuclear exchange. A recent study sponsored by the Royal United Services Institute in the UK concluded that cyber attacks are possible and that high-alert nuclear systems like ICBMs are likely the most vulnerable to such attacks.[17] Terrorists or other third parties are likely to seek to use cyber as a means to precipitate a crisis and facilitate miscalculation and possible nuclear use by interfering with such systems.

Nuclear non-proliferation

The 1968 NPT, which the US helped to establish, is a central element of the global nuclear-non-proliferation regime. Under Article VI of the NPT, all member states are obligated to:

> pursue negotiations in good faith on effective measures relating to cessation of the nuclear arms race at an early date and to nuclear disarmament, and on a treaty on general and complete disarmament under strict and effective international control.[18]

In addition, the final documents from the 2000 and 2010 NPT Review Conferences reaffirmed 'the unequivocal undertaking of the nuclear-weapon States to accomplish the total elimination of their nuclear arsenals leading to nuclear disarmament, to which all States parties are committed under article VI'.[19]

The 2009 report of the Congressional Commission on the Strategic Posture of the United States stated that 'it is clear that we cannot meet our goal of reducing the proliferation threat without substantial international cooperation'.[20] However, the same report warned that:

> cooperation of other nations increasingly depends on whether these nations perceive that the U.S. and Russia are moving to seriously reduce the salience of

nuclear weapons in their own force posture and are continuing to make significant reductions in their nuclear arsenal.[21]

NPT signatories will keenly watch the US decision regarding nuclear modernisation as an indicator of the US commitment to cutting its nuclear forces.

Views vary as to how the size, structure and declared posture of US nuclear forces influence the proliferation of nuclear weapons. Ultimately, there is an unsustainable political tension between the willingness of non-nuclear states to refrain indefinitely from acquiring nuclear weapons and the prolonged unwillingness of the nuclear-weapons states to eliminate their arsenals.[22] Since the mid-1980s the US and Russia have dramatically reduced the size of their nuclear arsenals. This progress towards their commitments to pursue disarmament, under Article VI of the NPT, is in danger of coming to a halt because of the lack of national plans or negotiated arms-control agreements to reduce arsenals below New START levels.[23] Without unambiguous commitments and concrete actions on the part of weapons-possessing states to reduce the role and size of their nuclear arsenals, the risk that non-nuclear states will seek to acquire such weapons increases.

The 2010 NPR stated a clear intention to avoid such an outcome:

> By working to reduce the salience of nuclear weapons in international affairs and moving step-by-step toward eliminating them, we can reverse the growing expectation that we are destined to live in a world with more nuclear-armed states, and decrease incentives for additional countries to hedge against an uncertain future by pursuing nuclear options of their own.[24]

The next opportunity to demonstrate progress on non-proliferation commitments within the NPT context is the treaty Review Conference scheduled for 2020. If the US does not reduce or curtail any of its current nuclear-force-modernisation programmes, its credibility on non-proliferation will be harmed. This will have negative consequences for its ability to persuade other countries to observe their own non-proliferation commitments or to join efforts to deny technology and materials to potential nuclear proliferators.

The choices the US makes are of paramount importance because the country is the first link in a chain of nuclear-armed states. US choices can have knock-on effects right down the chain, encouraging proliferation in states far removed from the strategic calculations of the US. For example, improvements in US capabilities can prompt changes in the size and posture of China's nuclear arsenal, which in turn bear directly on India's nuclear policy, which in turn influences Pakistan's nuclear-force-structure decisions.

The default US plan for renewal of the full triad does not demonstrate a willingness on the part of the United States to take the obligations of Article VI of the NPT and the 2010 Action Plan seriously. The 2010 Action Plan was agreed by consensus at the 2010 NPT Review Conference and contains a list of specific actions that nuclear-weapon states and non-nuclear-weapon states pledge to undertake.[25] The default US plan for renewal calls into doubt the commitment of the US to pursue nuclear disarmament as it provides for maintaining the current level of nuclear armament until 2080. The first alternative considered here, the streamlined triad, provides somewhat greater support for the global non-proliferation effort. The reductions to the number of strategic delivery vehicles, including fewer ICBMs and SLBMs, would allow the US to demonstrate a greater degree of commitment to both its obligations under NPT Article VI and progress towards reducing the arsenal that it maintained during the latter stages of the Cold War. If these reductions could somehow be made in the context of negotiated bilateral or reciprocal reduction to Russian nuclear forces, NPT objectives could be further advanced. However, in common with all nuclear-force options considered here, the US proposes to retain and modernise nuclear weapons during the next 30–40 years, which is inconsistent with the central objective of the NPT.

The streamlined triad would still produce incentives for other nations to retain, modernise and perhaps expand their nuclear arsenals. For example, the modest reduction to US ballistic-missile delivery systems compared with existing plans would be unlikely to reduce incentives for China to further expand its relatively small nuclear arsenal. China's nuclear capabilities exert influence on the proliferation decisions of many states including India, Indonesia, Japan, Malaysia, the Philippines, South Korea, Taiwan and Vietnam.

The air–sea dyad has several advantages with regard to efforts to prevent nuclear proliferation as compared with the two triad options. Cancellation of the LRSO missile and the mothballing of the ICBM leg of the strategic triad would demonstrate a significant change in the way the US thinks about nuclear weapons. Specifically, it would reduce the role of nuclear weapons in US strategy and embrace the concept that they exist only to deter nuclear use against the US or its allies. The ability of the US to launch a crippling first strike against Russia or China would be degraded, thus reducing incentives for vertical proliferation by Moscow and Beijing.[26] The unprecedented decision to retire an entire leg of the triad would dramatically strengthen the credibility and leadership of the US in the non-proliferation regime.

The major reductions to ballistic- and cruise-missile delivery systems required by the air–sea dyad option would indirectly reduce incentives for additional countries to acquire nuclear weapons. This is because China might slow or agree to cancel some of its nuclear-modernisation programmes in response to US reductions, particularly its current plan to deploy a ten-warhead heavy ICBM. While it might not be willing to cancel deployment of its heavy ICBM, it might agree to verifiable limits of three to four warheads per missile.

Willingness to cancel the LRSO missile and remove US forward-based nuclear weapons would strengthen the INF Treaty and potentially lead to further formal agreements with Russia on tactical nuclear weapons and a global ban on nuclear cruise missiles.[27] If Russia pulled back its forward-deployed tactical nuclear weapons in response to the US withdrawal, or as part of a new arms-control agreement, the chances of a terrorist acquisition of a nuclear weapon on the Russian side would also be diminished. The same would be true if Russia decided to scale back its ICBM modernisation plans in response to US retirement of the *Minuteman* force, for example by reducing *Sarmat* procurement or the number of warheads each new missile will carry.

An air–sea dyad option could put the US and its allies in stronger compliance with the NPT, bolster New START, improve the chances of resolving issues with the INF Treaty, and help sustain a moratorium on nuclear testing, as required by the 1996 Comprehensive Nuclear-Test-Ban Treaty (CTBT), which bans nuclear explosive testing. By removing 400 nuclear-armed ICBMs, two nuclear submarines and a nuclear cruise missile from the currently planned arsenal, the US would demonstrate convincingly that it valued the goal of the NPT and was honouring its commitments under Article VI, as well as the consensus documents from the 2000 and 2010 Review Conferences.

Specifically, the air–sea dyad reductions would demonstrate progress on the third action point of the 2010 plan:

> In implementing the unequivocal undertaking by
> the nuclear-weapon States to accomplish the total
> elimination of their nuclear arsenals, the nuclear-
> weapon States commit to undertake further efforts to
> reduce and ultimately eliminate all types of nuclear
> weapons, deployed and non-deployed, including
> through unilateral, bilateral, regional and multilateral
> measures.[28]

Like the air–sea dyad, the dispersed maritime dyad has several advantages for efforts to prevent nuclear proliferation. Eliminating the ICBM force and cancelling the LRSO would signal that the US views nuclear weapons solely for the purpose of deterring a nuclear attack. Phasing out the land-based missiles would significantly change US nuclear posture and reduce US ability to launch a debilitating first strike against Russia or China, thus reducing incentives for either state to seek further qualitative or quantitative proliferation.

The Comprehensive Nuclear-Test-Ban Treaty

The US government's default plan for replicating the full triad includes the introduction of interoperable warheads, which potentially poses a risk to the CTBT.[29] The concept envisions using parts from two different, existing warheads – a primary stage from the W87 ICBM warhead, and possibly a secondary stage from the W80 cruise-missile warhead – to make a new interoperable warhead. Those two parts of a two-stage warhead have never been used together, and such combinations have never been introduced into the nuclear US stockpile without explosive nuclear tests. However, the US no longer conducts such tests because it is a signatory to the CTBT, which is considered a pillar of the non-proliferation regime. In 2013 the Senate Appropriations Committee wrote that the concept 'may be unnecessarily complex and expensive, increase uncertainty about certification' and 'fail to address aging issues in a timely manner'.[30] The danger is that doubts may grow about the reliability of the interoperable warhead during its development, which can only be allayed by nuclear testing. This would contravene the testing moratorium and ruin prospects for the CTBT, as other nuclear powers would likely respond by conducting their own explosive testing.[31]

These threats to the CTBT are also inherent in the streamlined triad option. By contrast, the two dyad plans do not include the interoperable-warhead programme and so avoid the attendant threats to the CTBT and the global moratorium on testing by the principal nuclear powers. The two dyads also provide for cancellation of the LEPs for the W78 and W87 ICBM warheads. This would allow for simple LEPs for the two SLBM warheads, the W76-1 and W88. This could save an estimated US$30bn over 25 years and strengthen US pursuit of the objectives of the 2010 NPT Action Plan, which call for the eventual elimination of all types of nuclear weapons.

CHAPTER FIVE

Procurement trade-offs and support for conventional operations

A major consideration for the US is whether the expected outlay on full replacement of the nuclear triad is justified in the context of a finite defence budget, and the contribution that nuclear forces make to overall national defence priorities. The high expense and modest contribution to conventional operations are arguably the weakest aspects of the default plan for nuclear modernisation of the full triad. Funding the plan within the limitations of projected defence budgets will require DoD officials to delay or cut back purchases of conventional weaponry and other military capabilities deemed essential to US security.

Opportunity costs

According to projections by the Pentagon and independent organisations, major conventional military programmes will need to be cut during the next 30 years in order to fully cover the US$1-trillion cost of the planned modernisation of nuclear forces. This creates the risk of shortfalls in funding for conventional US military capabilities in the coming decades.

Officials from the US Air Force have claimed that after 2020, funding levels for its conventional combat, refuelling, transport and reconnaissance aircraft will become 'unmanageable' if nuclear-weapons systems called for under the full triad plan are acquired.[1] In the 2020s, the Air Force plans to begin full-rate production of the F-35 multi-role attack fighter, the KC-46 refuelling tanker and several unmanned aircraft, as well as the B-21 strategic bomber. These programmes account for 99% of its acquisition budget and will crowd out all other procurement programmes and consume a large proportion of research and development budgets for subsequent years.[2]

With respect to Navy programmes, Pentagon budget officials are concerned that spending on the *Columbia*-class submarines will force cutbacks to conventional shipbuilding programmes, principally the new *Virginia*-class attack submarines, *Ford*-class aircraft carriers and new fleets of destroyers that make vital contributions to US military power across the spectrum of conflict from intelligence collection and special operations to full-scale regional conflict. Cutbacks in these programmes could also severely degrade the country's conventional shipbuilding industrial base.[3]

Conventional ground forces such as those that deter aggression against US allies in Europe and Asia, and undertake operations against the Islamic State, also known as ISIS or ISIL, in Syria and Iraq, could also be short-changed by a maximalist approach to nuclear modernisation. US conventional military support for NATO and East Asian allies is another crucial capability that nuclear-weapon spending could adversely affect. These regions face primarily conventional military challenges from Russia and China and a combined nuclear–conventional threat from North Korea. Achieving relatively small savings by downsizing current nuclear-modernisation plans could provide resources for additional combat brigades to NATO that could boost deterrence in the Baltic region or Eastern Europe.

The proposed streamlined triad will cost an estimated US$691bn over 30 years, yielding a saving of US$272bn compared with the existing plan for a full triad.[4] This level of savings is significant, but it does not eliminate the need to make trade-offs in existing defence-procurement priorities because it does not cover the projected shortfall in defence budgets. Projected shortfall for only the next five years, FY2017–FY2021, is US$130bn.[5] Some of the highest spending years for the streamlined triad modernisation plan will be during 2021–35, when shortfalls will dramatically increase.

Therefore, while slightly more fiscally responsible than the full triad, the streamlined triad would also require defence strategists to delay or cut back purchases of conventional weaponry and spending on other military capabilities. Like the current plan, this would impact Air Force acquisition of several conventional and combat-support aircraft as well as the Navy's long-term conventional shipbuilding plans. Other joint capabilities like special-operation forces, precision global strike, intelligence, surveillance and reconnaissance (ISR), and research and development would have to be weighed against the priorities of nuclear modernisation. Trade-offs between defence and non-defence expenditures that influence US security within the overall federal budget would also be necessary.

An air–sea dyad strategic modernisation programme would require at least 30 years to complete and cost an estimated US$531bn, representing a saving of US$432bn over 30 years compared with current plans – a reduction of almost 45% in the estimated cost of modernising the US nuclear arsenal.[6] To a greater extent than either of the triad options, the air–sea dyad acknowledges that nuclear deterrence is only one of several major national-security priorities. By generating major savings, this option would greatly relieve pressure on defence strategists to delay or cut back spending on conventional weaponry and other military capabilities, including on conventional aircraft and shipbuilding. The air–sea dyad would allow more spending on modernised ground forces, counter-terrorism, non-proliferation, missile defence, space defence, cyber security and providing stronger support for US allies in Asia and Europe. It would also reduce the need to make trade-offs between defence and non-defence expenditures that influence US security within the overall federal budget.

One example of how the air–sea dyad or similar scaled-back nuclear-modernisation programmes could contribute to other defence priorities concerns the challenges facing NATO. A notable RAND study predicted in 2015 that NATO forces could not currently prevent a Russian invasion of the Baltic states, and that a NATO force of about seven brigades, including three heavy armoured brigades, would be needed to repel such an attack. Creating and maintaining such a force, RAND estimated, might cost around US$2.7bn per year.[7] Put in perspective, the estimated US$30bn the Pentagon would save just by cancelling the LRSO under the air–sea dyad plan could sustain conventional forces in the Baltic region at a level sufficient to achieve conventional deterrence and defence for more than a decade.

A dispersed maritime dyad strategic modernisation programme would require at least 30 years to complete and cost an estimated US$520bn, representing a saving of US$443bn over 30 years compared with the current plan.[8] Like the other dyad option, this level of savings would obviate the need to slow or cancel any of the planned conventional-weapons procurement programmes during the next 30 years and leave significant resources for other defence priorities such as counter-terrorism, cyber security and modernised ground forces.

Under the air–sea dyad and the dispersed maritime dyad, there would be significant changes to existing plans to extend the life of nuclear warheads. The W80-4 cruise-missile warhead would be cancelled, and the retirement of the ICBM force by 2030 would obviate the need for the proposed interoperable warhead. The W78 and W87 ICBM warheads could be retired or placed in storage. The W88 and W76-1 SLBM warheads could undergo traditional life extension as needed sometime after 2030 and then be placed on refurbished *Trident* II missiles aboard the *Columbia*-class submarines.

The need for fewer warheads and warhead types mean that both dyad modernisation options would also reduce infrastructure and stockpile-maintenance costs to some degree. A pit-manufacturing capability of 50–80 pits per year is already in excess of what is needed to maintain a stockpile supporting the current modernisation plan, which provides for the retention of seven warhead types and approximately 4,000 total active warheads. If the active stockpile was reduced to 2,500 weapons of three or four warhead types (B61-12, W80-4, W76-1 and W88), the need for total pit operations per year to maintain the stockpile would be reduced further. Reserve W76 and W88 pits could be re-used and the surplus pits that would result from the retirement of the W80-1, W78 and W87 could act as an additional strategic reserve or 'hedge'.

However, some would argue that the need for a 'surge' or 'hedge' pit-manufacturing capability would increase because of the possibility that a flaw in one warhead type would be discovered that might require replacement of the entire inventory of that type. Therefore, the precise cost saving and reduction to the nuclear-warhead supply chain cannot be accurately estimated with open-source information because the details surrounding nuclear-component inventories and industrial operations is highly classified. One cannot say definitively, for example, that moving to dyad options would obviate the need for *any* new factory space for pit manufacturing, but it is possible that this would be the case.

To the greatest extent of all the cases, the dispersed maritime dyad option acknowledges that nuclear deterrence is only one of several major national-security priorities. This option would allow the most spending on counter-terrorism, non-proliferation, missile defence, space defence, cyber security, biosecurity, research and development, and support for US allies in Europe and Asia. Like the other dyad option, it would also reduce the need to make trade-offs between defence and non-defence expenditures that influence US security within the overall federal budget.

Support for conventional operations

All four nuclear-modernisation options considered in this book will take several decades to implement. Given the rapidly evolving global security environment it is unlikely that a nuclear force based on the current triad will be an optimal force structure for this entire period. Yet this is what the full triad option and, to a large extent, the streamlined triad envision. Developments in the last 20 years suggest that the threats of regional conflict, nuclear terrorism, information-centric warfare and cyber tactics will increase. A trillion-dollar investment in US defence forces during the next 30 years based on the 60-year-old model of today's nuclear triad runs the risk of being an ineffective deterrent against future threats. Instead, large, long-term investment in strategic forces should provide flexible, adaptive capabilities across a broad spectrum of defence needs and not single-purpose platforms designed and dedicated only to nuclear missions.

New design philosophies could provide significant advantages to the next generation of US strategic forces. One such philosophy is to maximise the contribution that expensive, long-service-life, nuclear-weapon platforms can make to non-nuclear military operations ('designing for denuclearisation'). This strategy would attach less value to single-purpose delivery systems such as nuclear-armed ICBMs and more value to multi-purpose assets such as strategic aircraft, dual-capable naval platforms and ISR capabilities that are designed to support both nuclear and non-nuclear missions.

In terms of the construction of nuclear-weapon systems, this design philosophy seeks to optimise the ability of major dual-capable platforms to contribute to non-nuclear missions and their ability to be converted to solely non-nuclear missions as the future security environment allows. It also attempts to anticipate or 'offset' defence-technology trends that could increase the vulnerability of US nuclear-delivery systems or prevent them from executing missions in disputed battlespace.

The planned full triad will make important but moderate contributions to conventional military operations. It retains, at great expense, two legs of the triad that are almost exclusively single-purpose nuclear platforms. The ICBMs and the *Columbia*-class SSBNs make little contribution to US conventional military operations. The submarines make modest contributions such as communications and passive signals-intelligence collection, but their primary mission is to remain undetected and invulnerable in their patrol areas. The ICBMs in their current and planned configuration are a nuclear-only system. The bomber leg, with its manned crew, multifunction sensors and communications, inherent dual-payload capability, and ability to deploy to dozens of air bases around the world, is clearly the leg of the nuclear triad most integrated with US conventional forces.

There is little difference between the streamlined triad and full triad with regard to the contribution to conventional operations and capabilities. Both commit major resources to nuclear-only systems. Similarly, both options plan for the procurement of 100 B-21 strategic aircraft, the system that contributes the most to conventional capabilities. Under all four modernisation options, only 50 or fewer of these new planes would be equipped to deliver nuclear weapons.

The air–sea dyad eliminates one nuclear-only leg of the existing triad that makes no significant contribution to conventional operations. Its submarine force would make a limited contribution to conventional operations, along the lines discussed above, while the 80-strong strategic bomber force would make a greater contribution – albeit perhaps less so than in the case of the 100-strong bomber forces provided for under the triad options.

The dispersed maritime dyad is the only option that can make unique contributions to conventional military operations. This is because it includes the purchase of eight additional *Virginia*-class submarines that would be equipped for both nuclear and conventional operations. These submarines, each armed with four nuclear ballistic missiles plus conventional anti-ship and land-attack cruise missiles, as well as special-operations and intelligence-gathering capabilities, would offer diverse and flexible capabilities in conventional conflicts.

CONCLUSION

This book has assessed the US plan for nuclear modernisation and three alternatives against a range of criteria: deterrent power and flexibility; strategic stability and arms control; nuclear security and non-proliferation; and trade-offs with conventional procurement as well as contributions to conventional operations. All the modernisation plans would meet the requirements of deterrence against nuclear-armed states. On the other criteria, the existing plan fares less well, in large part because it replicates the Cold War triad despite enormous changes in the strategic context.

The full triad plan and its alternatives

Although the default plan's force structure is compliant with New START, it threatens crisis and arms-race stability with Russia by enhancing capabilities that – in tandem with advanced US conventional weapons and ballistic-missile defence – exacerbate Russian concerns that the US intends to negate Moscow's nuclear deterrent. It contains weapons systems that can destabilise the nuclear balance and create incentives for potential adversaries to place their nuclear forces on higher alert status and increase their nuclear war-fighting capability. For example, US plans to continue improving the hard-target-kill capabilities of US nuclear warheads and to deploy the B61-12 guided bomb and a nuclear-armed LRSO are further stoking Russian threat perceptions. This could prompt reciprocal deployments of new Russian nuclear-armed air- and ground-launched cruise missiles. The risk increases if the US deploys the thousands of conventional long-range cruise missiles it is purchasing.[1] Russia has not matched the United States' development of very precise and highly destructive conventional weapons, together with ballistic-missile defences, and these alter the strategic balance between the two states.

The planned capability increases under the current plan, against the background of a changed strategic balance, undermine crisis and arms-race stability in the US relationships with China as well as Russia. They also represent a threat to the extension of the New START agreement and to the preservation of the INF Treaty, because they increase the risk of Russia calculating that it can only achieve security by releasing itself from the limitations that these agreements impose. Russian violations of the INF Treaty, while limited at this point, may be an indication of this calculation. Of the four modernisation plans, the full triad is the most likely to encourage Russia to follow a path of nuclear modernisation that will threaten the security of the US and its allies.

Moreover, the full triad does not adequately take into account the increased threats to the security of US nuclear weapons in Europe, where bases are not sufficiently secure, and in the US where STRATCOM has admitted it is worried about the risk of cyber attack against the ICBM force. With regard to US commitments under the NPT and the global non-proliferation effort, the full triad plan is a threat because it proposes to retain roughly the same US nuclear force for decades to come. Given that progress towards strategic arms reduction has ground to a halt since the 1990s, this threat is significant. In light of the growing frustration among non-nuclear-weapon states over the failure of the P5 to make progress on nuclear disarmament, the current plan is a risky course. US security interests are best served by supporting global non-proliferation efforts, not by losing a leadership role in this sphere by weakening efforts to reduce the role of nuclear weapons in US security strategy.

Certain elements of the current modernisation programme may do major damage to nuclear non-proliferation efforts. For example, the proposed interoperable warhead created from parts from two existing warheads is unprecedented; until now, all such warheads have been tested but this one has not been. Without testing, there will be some doubt regarding its reliability, and certification might be a problem. The only definitive way to overcome these potential hurdles would be an explosive test, but this would break the global moratorium on explosive testing by the established nuclear powers. It would also likely lead to the unravelling of the 1996 CTBT.

Finally, the expense of replacing the full triad is such that a number of major planned procurements of conventional systems appear untenable, and will either have to be shelved or more likely delayed or whittled down. These include major naval-combat vessels such as cruisers, destroyers and attack submarines, and new fighter and tanker aircraft. Another possible negative consequence of the high cost is that insufficient funds could mean that the planned number of new platforms is sharply reduced in an uncoordinated manner, resulting in an imbalanced force. The completion of only 20 B-2 bombers when at one time 132 were planned should serve as a cautionary tale. Fiscal constraints were largely responsible for such a dramatic curtailment of the full complement of B-2 aircraft, with the result that STRATCOM has had to rely on extending use of the B-52 and B-1 well beyond their expected service lives.

The streamlined triad is New START-compliant, and the reduction in the number of ICBMs and SSBNs acknowledges the changed strategic context with Russia and should go some way towards easing Russian concerns about US intentions (specifically whether the US intends to negate Russia's deterrent in the event of a conflict). Yet it is open to doubt whether the cuts would go far enough to achieve this objective, given that this option includes three of the most contentious elements of the current modernisation plan: the B61-12 bomb, to be deployed in Europe; the LRSO; and hard-target-killing warheads, which together with advanced conventional weaponry and ballistic-missile defence would form a new triad that Russia could perceive as a plan to achieve strategic primacy. Therefore, even the streamlined triad might make it difficult to extend New START, preserve the INF Treaty, and avoid a new nuclear-arms race with Russia and perhaps China.

With regard to nuclear security, the streamlined triad differs little from the full triad plan. It continues the trend of underfunding domestic and international nuclear-security and material-protection programmes. It proposes to deploy a significant number of nuclear bombs in Europe, where their security cannot be guaranteed. And it retains the ICBM force, which is vulnerable to cyber attack. The reduction in platforms and warheads under the streamlined triad might buy the US some breathing space in its dealings with non-nuclear states over its Article VI commitment under the NPT. However, the cuts do not amount to a determined move in the direction of disarmament, and the planned introduction of the interoperable warhead constitutes a threat to the CTBT and the global moratorium on nuclear testing by major powers.

The reduced cost of the streamlined triad, as compared with existing plans, would ease some of the funding strains on planned conventional procurements. However, the savings would not be sufficient to avoid the need for tax increases, spending cuts elsewhere, or significant delays or downgrades to non-nuclear procurement plans. As with the full triad, the plan would only make modest contributions to conventional operations and capabilities.

The air–sea dyad eliminates the redundancy offered by the ICBM force and presents a radical departure from the nuclear arsenal of the past few decades. It would also weaken the United States' ability to launch a counterforce strike against Russia. This option would be New START-compliant and more likely to preserve strategic stability than the triad options. The elimination of the ICBM leg, preferably through negotiations with Russia, would send a strong signal that the US did not intend to negate Russia's deterrent power.

To a greater extent than the triad options, this dyad would acknowledge the changed strategic context in US–Russian relations, with the US having made advances in conventional precision weaponry and ballistic-missile defence that Russia has not matched. These significant changes undeniably affect Russia's strategic calculus. The absence from the air–sea dyad of plans to deploy the B61-12 guided bomb in Europe, and the decision to cancel the LRSO, would also improve arms-race and crisis stability. As a consequence of these developments, the chance of New START being extended would be improved. Furthermore, the likelihood would increase that discussions could begin on preserving the INF Treaty and negotiating a new treaty covering tactical nuclear weapons that formalised withdrawal of US nuclear weapons from NATO bases and required storage of Russian tactical nuclear weapons away from Europe.

In the nuclear-security sphere, the elimination of the ICBM force from 2030 would ease fears over the hacking of land-based missiles and a resultant unintentional nuclear exchange or accident. The decision to base the B61-12 bombs in the US, rather than deploying them to Turkey and Western Europe, would most likely reduce the risks of theft or sabotage. Scrapping ICBMs would deliver a fillip to the global non-proliferation effort and confirm the United States' leadership role in this arena. Cancelling the interoperable warhead would also avoid the US potentially facing a dilemma about warhead reliability that would threaten the CTBT.

The air–sea dyad would be much cheaper than the existing modernisation plan, saving US$432bn over 30 years and so eliminating most of the trade-offs between nuclear and conventional platforms and systems that the DoD would otherwise have to make in its procurement plans. However, this dyad would make a very modest contribution to conventional operations and capabilities.

The dispersed maritime dyad goes further still in reducing the number of warheads in the US arsenal, although that number could be increased in shorter order if the need arose. Without the ICBM leg, the force would have less redundancy but would remain large and flexible enough, and sufficiently survivable, to maintain deterrence against China and Russia, even allowing for those states' planned nuclear modernisations. No adversary could reasonably hope to destroy the expanded submarine force in a surprise attack, and a sizeable number of strategic bombers would also survive.

This second dyad option is New START-compliant, with room to spare. It would go a long way towards reassuring Moscow that the US did not intend to escape from its relationship of mutual vulnerability with Russia. Without the US ICBM force, Russian concerns about the survivability of its own ICBMs would be greatly eased. Cancelling the LRSO and keeping the B61-12 out of Europe would further under-pin arms-race and crisis stability. Against this background, the prospects for the extension of New START and preservation of the INF Treaty would be healthy. Initiating talks with Russia to limit or reduce tactical nuclear weapons might also become possible.

The benefits of the dispersed maritime dyad for nuclear security and non-proliferation initiatives are substantial. As with the air–sea dyad, it eliminates the cyber-vulnerable ICBM force and keeps nuclear bombs out of potentially insecure bases in Turkey and Europe. The boost to the global non-prolif-eration effort, and the US leadership role within it, would be considerable.

Like the other dyad, this option would yield consider-able financial savings, estimated at US$443bn over 30 years compared with the full triad. Those savings could be ploughed into much-needed conventional procurement and operations. Moreover, the dispersed maritime dyad would make unique, considerable contributions to conventional operations through its enlarged submarine force of SSBNs and SSNs, as well as through the bomber force.

An examination of the four plans against the criteria for nuclear modernisation leads to the conclusion that a triad of independent means of delivering nuclear weapons is not essential for a credible and reliable deterrent for the US and its allies. Strategic stability only requires that US nuclear forces can survive any attempt to destroy them and still inflict unac-ceptable damage on the attacker. US nuclear forces currently have this capability, and recent Pentagon analysis confirmed that even complete fulfilment of Russia and China's nuclear-modernisation plans during the next 10–15 years would not negate it.[2] This is largely because of the US fleet of *Ohio*-class ballistic-missile submarines and their planned replacement with the *Columbia*-class SSBNs from 2030. All of the modernisation plans presented here would preserve the submarine leg.

Phasing out the ICBM force, as proposed by both dyad options, would have significant advantages with regard to the preservation of strategic stability in US relations with Russia. It would reduce the ability of the US to launch a degrading counterforce strike against Russia's land-based missiles, which are the centrepiece of its nuclear force. This would offer Russia reassurance that the US was not seeking to negate its deterrent, and Russia would therefore be less likely to develop or posture its own nuclear force in ways the US would find destabilising. The elimination of ICBMs would also be positive from a security standpoint, as they are the element of the triad most vulnerable to a cyber attack that could cause an accident or incident that precipitates a nuclear exchange.

A decision to switch from the currently planned full triad to a dyad structure would unlock huge savings for the defence budget over a 30-year period. That in turn would enable the US to proceed with the planned procurement of a range of military platforms that would fulfil identified needs but may not be affordable given the costs of nuclear modernisation. Moreover, by making savings on the nuclear force, the US would be in a stronger position to invest money in a range of nuclear-security initiatives at home and abroad, thus rising to the challenge of non-state actors such as ISIS or al-Qaeda seeking to obtain a nuclear weapon.

The US should embrace two innovative design philosophies in its nuclear-modernisation planning. The first, which recognises the salience of arms control, is 'designing for denuclearisation'. It is based on the assumption that US strategy will continue to place a high value on nuclear non-proliferation, reducing the threat of nuclear terrorism and the eventual elimination of nuclear weapons. In essence, designing for denuclearisation would be similar to a hedge strategy because it would seek to provide US nuclear-weapons infrastructure and operational forces with characteristics that could facilitate verified arms-control agreements, increase transparency, improve strategic stability and simplify conversion to non-nuclear missions.

The two dyad options are more consistent with this approach than the triad options. The removal of ICBMs from silos could be verified easily using satellite or other airborne imagery, and under the dispersed maritime dyad the nuclear missiles could be easily removed from *Virginia*-class SSNs and the boats would require only minor modification to be certified as conventional-only platforms. In addition, if the security environment improved, completing the construction of unfinished *Virginia*-class boats as non-nuclear weapon platforms would be less costly.

The second design philosophy is to maximise the contribution that expensive, long-service-life nuclear-weapon platforms can make to non-nuclear military operations. It also attempts to anticipate or offset defence-technology trends that can increase the vulnerability of US nuclear-delivery systems or prevent them from executing missions in disputed battlespace. Some of these trends include improvements to air defences, sensor and target-tracking capabilities, and the accuracy and responsiveness of offensive weaponry. These advances could make even SLBMs more vulnerable. One response that hedges against this trend is to increase the number of the least-vulnerable nuclear platforms. The planned full triad makes only modest contributions to these goals despite its very high cost. The two dyad options envision phasing out nuclear-only ICBMs and minimising the nuclear role of strategic aircraft while maximising their conventional capabilities. Only the dispersed maritime dyad increases the number of currently invulnerable nuclear-delivery vehicles.

Justifying nuclear reductions at a time of strategic tension

The three alternative nuclear-modernisation options considered in this study all represent reductions of the full triad option, which is the current US/NATO plan. Why would US and allied decision-makers support a scaled-back nuclear-modernisation plan at a time of strategic tension with potential adversaries, including Russia and China? There are several reasons, one of which is the potential contribution that nuclear restraint may make to reducing strategic tension and strengthening stability.

Strategic relations and the future balance of nuclear forces among the US, Russia and China are currently strained and uncertain. This increases the chances of misperception and fuels worst-case assessments regarding competitor intentions and capabilities. The result is a spiral of mistrust and greater incentives for arms-racing, with its attendant costs and risks.[3] Escaping this dynamic is in the mutual interests of all three states.

During the Cold War, the US and the Soviet Union sometimes sought to improve relations through strategic arms negotiations, even at times of tension. For example, the negotiations that culminated in the 1987 INF Treaty began during one of the tensest periods of the Cold War. They resulted in the mutual curtailment of major nuclear-weapons deployments in the European theatre and the elimination of hundreds of cruise and ballistic missiles with ranges of 500–5,500km.

In the last five years, strategic dialogue between Russia and the US has deteriorated and both countries are engaged in extensive nuclear-force modernisation programmes. Elements of these programmes, including extremely accurate tactical nuclear weapons, MIRVed ICBMs and missile defences, will make the strategic balance more dynamic and unpredictable, even if New START is extended in 2021. If Washington can cut back its nuclear-modernisation plans in coordination with Moscow, it could help build confidence and improve arms-race and crisis stability. In other words, a new anticipatory nuclear arms-control treaty could resolve pressing security problems for both states and help to stabilise the relationship. Such an outcome could also have a positive spillover effect on Chinese modernisation plans.

Another reason the US should support scaled-back nuclear-modernisation plans is to achieve the potential strategic and political benefits outlined in the analysis of the four options. These include improved standing within the non-proliferation regime, particularly among the non-nuclear-weapon states, and a slightly reduced risk of nuclear terrorism. The US could significantly reduce the risk of nuclear terrorism by withdrawing nuclear weapons from NATO bases, as called for by the two dyad options. Likewise, the risk of a cyber attack on the US nuclear arsenal would be reduced if the most vulnerable leg of the triad, the ICBMs, was retired – another requirement of the dyad options.

The non-proliferation benefits of nuclear-modernisation restraint are potentially significant, even if Russia did not immediately reciprocate. Pursuit of a streamlined triad, an air–sea dyad or a dispersed maritime dyad would progressively put the US on a stronger footing with respect to the NPT Review Conferences scheduled for 2020 and beyond. Any of these alternatives to the full triad plan would also help the US show that it was meeting its obligations under Article VI of the NPT. For example, a US announcement that it was moving to a force of 1,000–1,100 deployed nuclear warheads despite Russian modernisation plans would clearly set it apart from all nations that are continuing to expand their nuclear arsenals. This would put Washington in a position of leadership in the non-proliferation regime, pressure others to follow suit and advance the Prague agenda articulated by then-president Obama in 2009. The simultaneous announcement of programmes to strengthen NATO's conventional defence capabilities would indicate continuing US commitment to NATO defence and reduce any pressure NATO states might feel to procure their own nuclear forces in light of US nuclear reductions.

Considerations regarding the allocation of finite defence resources may also motivate the US to implement nuclear reductions during times of strategic tension. This study has made clear the trade-offs that the US must make between spending on nuclear forces and conventional military capabilities. A prime example is the concern over the relative strength of Russian conventional forces compared with those of NATO. A more effective means for NATO to deter Russian conventional aggression against the Baltic states or Poland is to improve its own conventional forces. If the US fully funds its default nuclear-modernisation plan, it will have fewer resources available to spend on strengthening NATO's conventional forces. Trying to deter potential Russian conventional attacks with a new generation of nuclear warheads and delivery vehicles entails more risk than diverting sufficient resources towards strengthening NATO's conventional forces.

To capture these potential gains, the US should seek to negotiate mutual reductions with Russia. Washington has strategic space to safely consider such options. US DoD analysis of Russian nuclear forces, conducted in coordination with the director of national intelligence and sent to Congress in May 2012, concluded that even the worst-case scenario of a Russian surprise attack on the US arsenal would have 'little to no effect' on the United States' ability to retaliate with a devastating strike against Russia. This would be the case even if the

US remained in compliance with the New START Treaty while Russia did not.[4]

In summary, despite the current period of strategic tension with Russia and, to a lesser extent, China, the US and NATO still have sound reasons to consider alternative nuclear-modernisation plans. The potential benefits outlined above are certainly more likely if Russia and China respond positively and in kind to US modernisation restraint. That in turn is more likely if constructive strategic dialogues can be established and maintained with both states. If the US declares a willingness to be flexible on nuclear modernisation and seeks creative antici-patory arms-control efforts, possibly including the withdrawal of US nuclear arms from Europe, it might be able to establish a strategic dialogue with Russia. China's arsenal is still small compared with that of the US, so alternative, scaled-back modernisation plans by Washington have no risk of providing Beijing with strategic advantage for the foreseeable future.

Don't overpay or overplay

The US should carefully assess proposals by former secretary of defense William Perry and former head of STRATCOM and vice chairman of the Joint Chiefs of Staff James Cartwright to reduce the scope of nuclear-modernisation plans. Specifically, both officials declared that a force of 1,000 or fewer deployed nuclear weapons would be sufficient for deterrence for decades to come.[5] They also suggested that the ICBM leg of the triad is unnecessary and that its retirement would yield strategic and fiscal advantages.

The two dyad modernisation options comfortably meet the threshold for effective deterrence identified in the 2013 Report on Nuclear Employment Strategy, which concluded that the US could effectively maintain nuclear deterrence for decades with an arsenal approximately one-third smaller than the current force of 1,550 warheads under New START. Nuclear-modernisation plans that envision a smaller nuclear arsenal with reductions formalised and verified through new arms-control agreements with Russia and perhaps other nations will best serve the national-security interests of the US and its allies.

The cost and significant drawbacks of existing plans to renew the US nuclear arsenal are such that alternatives should be carefully considered. The three alternatives presented here are by no means exhaustive but they outline a few options along a spectrum. They also highlight some of the most problematic aspects of the full triad modernisation plan, which should be avoided. These alternatives take into account the projected nuclear-modernisation plans of Russia and China in the next few decades and include the capability to rapidly expand the number of deliverable warheads if called for by unanticipated changes in the security environment. This can be done by adding additional warheads to long-range missiles, primarily those on submarines, and by deploying reserve warheads currently in storage for delivery by aircraft.

The advantages of the alternatives in terms of strategic stability, consistency with guidance, nuclear security, non-proliferation, savings that can be directed to non-nuclear platforms, and support for conventional operations are considerable. Yet decision-makers might well hesitate to commit to a smaller force for fear that it would weaken deterrence.

It is worth recalling, therefore, that a smaller force could still have enormous destructive power that would be sufficient to maintain deterrence. All three alternative plans would give the US a large, diverse, flexible and responsive nuclear arsenal that would provide the president with multiple options for employing nuclear weapons. Hundreds of nuclear warheads of varying destructive yield (from a fraction of a kiloton to more than 400 kilotons) would be available for use even after the US suffered an attack by Russia, its strongest potential adversary. All of the force-structure options provide the means for limited and discriminate nuclear strikes in any worldwide region. At very low levels of nuclear employment (between one and three nuclear weapons of less than ten kilotons) by adversaries with small nuclear forces, the US retains and is dramatically expanding its ability to strike effectively and limit damage with missile defences and non-nuclear weapons.

APPENDIX

Figure 6: **US strategic nuclear weapons, 1960–90**

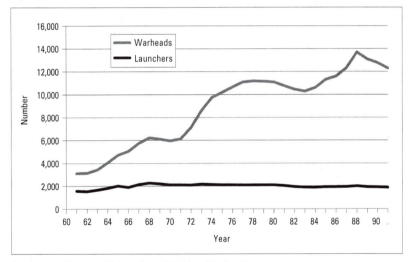

Source: Natural Resources Defense Council, Archive of Nuclear Data

Figure 7: **US strategic nuclear forces, 1991–2016**

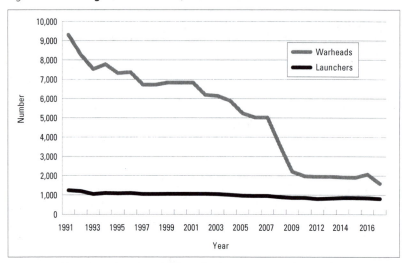

Source: Natural Resources Defense Council, Archive of Nuclear Data, Bulletin of Atomic Scientists, Nuclear Notebook

NOTES

Introduction

1 See Jon Wolfsthal, Jeffrey Lewis and Marc Quint, *The Trillion Dollar Nuclear Triad* (Monterey, CA: James Martin Center for Nonproliferation Studies, January 2014), https://www.nonproliferation.org/wp-content/uploads/2016/04/140107_trillion_dollar_nuclear_triad.pdf.

2 US and Russian strategic aircraft may carry up to 20 nuclear weapons, but for the purposes of the New START Treaty, they are counted as one warhead.

3 For detailed estimates of US and Russian nuclear forces see the *FAS Nuclear Notebook*, https://fas.org/issues/nuclear-weapons/nuclear-notebook/, particularly Hans M. Kristensen and Robert S. Norris, 'Russian Nuclear Forces, 2015', *Bulletin of the Atomic Scientists*, vol. 71, no. 3, pp. 84–97; and Hans M. Kristensen and Robert S. Norris, 'Russian Nuclear Forces, 2015', *Bulletin of the Atomic Scientists*, vol. 71, no. 2, pp. 107–19.

4 See US Congress, House Armed Forces, Strategic Forces, Hearing on the Proposed Fiscal 2014 Defense Authorization as it Relates to Atomic Energy Defense Activities, 113th Congress, 1st session, 9 May 2013; and US Department of Defense, 'Report on Nuclear Employment Strategy of the United States Specified in Section 491 of 10 U.S.C.', 2013, http://www.globalsecurity.org/wmd/library/policy/dod/us-nuclear-employment-strategy.pdf, p. 5. See also US Department of Defense, '2014 Quadrennial Defense Review', March 2014, http://archive.defense.gov/pubs/2014_Quadrennial_Defense_Review.pdf; and US Department of Defense 'National Security Strategy', February 2015, http://nssarchive.us/wp-content/uploads/2015/02/2015.pdf.

5 Congressional Budget Office, 'Projected Costs of U.S. Nuclear Forces, 2017 to 2026', February 2017, https://www.cbo.gov/publication/52401.

6 Wolfsthal, Lewis and Quint, *The Trillion Dollar Nuclear Triad*.

7 Estimates are consistent with Congressional Budget Office, 'Projected Costs of U.S. Nuclear Forces, 2017 to 2026', and Department of Energy, National Nuclear Security Administration, 'FY 2016

Congressional Budget Request', vol. 1, February 2015, http://energy.gov/sites/prod/files/2015/02/f19/FY2016BudgetVolume1_1.pdf. In general, this report relies on data from the annual budget process, supplemented by reports prepared by the Congressional Budget Office, the Government Accountability Office and congressional testimony. In some cases, the compiled estimates are supplemented with historical cost data. Estimates are restricted to costs directly tied to nuclear weapons and their delivery systems. They do not include related programmes such as system dismantlement, nuclear-material disposal or environmental remediation, intelligence expenditures related to nuclear missions and targeting, or missile defence.

8   US Department of Defense, 'Increasing Transparency in the U.S. Nuclear Weapons Stockpile', 3 May 2010, https://www.defense.gov/Portals/1/features/defenseReviews/NPR/10-05-03_Fact_Sheet_US_Nuclear_Transparency__FINAL_w_Date.pdf.

9   Hans M. Kristensen and Robert S. Norris, 'United States Nuclear Forces, 2016', *Bulletin of the Atomic Scientists*, vol. 72, no. 2, pp. 63–73.

10 Todd Harrison, 'Defense Modernization Plans Through the 2020s: Addressing the Bow Wave', Center for Strategic and International Studies, January 2016, p. 31, http://csis.org/files/publication/160126_Harrison_DefenseModernization_Web.pdf.

11 Remarks by then-president Barack Obama, Hradcany Square, Prague, Czech Republic, 5 April 2009, http://www.huffingtonpost.com/2009/04/05/obama-prague-speech-on-

nu_n_183219.html. See also the Nuclear Security Project launched by Sam Nunn, George Schultz, William Perry and Henry Kissinger, http://www.nti.org/about/projects/nuclear-security-project/.

12 Obama, remarks made in Prague.

13 See Harold A. Feiveson (ed.), *The Nuclear Turning Point: A Blueprint for Deep Cuts and De-Alerting of Nuclear Weapons* (Washington DC, Brookings Institution Press, 1999); and William J. Perry, *My Journey at the Nuclear Brink* (Stanford, CA: Stanford University Press, 2015).

14 Sustaining nuclear deterrence with the minimum number of warheads in the stockpile is a principle with broad currency in the nuclear-policy world. Some of the advocates of this position include Gen. (Retd) James Cartwright, former commander of US Strategic Command, who in 2012 outlined a proposed nuclear posture consisting of only 450 deployed warheads. See 'Modernizing U.S. Nuclear Strategy, Force Structure and Posture', Global Zero U.S. Nuclear Policy Commission Report, May 2012. Likewise, Air University scholars Gary Schaub Jr and James Wood Forsyth Jr have noted, 'America's nuclear security can rest easily on a relatively small number of counterforce and countervalue weapons totaling just over 300.' See James Wood Forsyth Jr, B. Chance Saltzman and Gary Schaub Jr, 'Remembrance of Things Past: The Enduring Value of Nuclear Weapons', *Strategic Studies Quarterly*, Spring 2010, pp. 74–89. Finally, in June 2013, then-president Obama announced his conviction that the United States could reduce its deployed nuclear stockpile by one-third while still

maintaining the credibility of US deterrence and ensuring the security of US allies. See 'Remarks by President Obama at the Brandenburg Gate', Berlin, Germany, 19 June 2013, https://obamawhitehouse.archives.gov/the-press-office/2013/06/19/remarks-president-obama-brandenburg-gate-berlin-germany.

[15] Details of the 3+2 concept are provided in the sections on nuclear warheads in Chapter One.

Chapter One

[1] Tony Capaccio, 'U.S. Bomber Planes at $81 Billion Seen 47% More Than Plan', Bloomberg, 6 December 2013, http://www.bloomberg.com/news/articles/2013-12-06/u-s-bombers-seen-costing-81-billion-47-more-than-plan.

[2] Presentation to Senate Armed Services Committee Subcommittee on Strategic Forces, United States Senate, Subject: ICBMs, Helicopters, Cruise Missiles, Bombers And Warheads, statement of Major-General Roger Burg (Af/A3s), 28 March 2007.

[3] Hans M. Kristensen, 'LRSO: The Nuclear Cruise Missile Mission', Federation of American Scientists Strategic Security blog, 20 October 2015, https://fas.org/blogs/security/2015/10/lrso-mission/.

[4] Hans M. Kristensen and Robert S. Norris, 'United States Nuclear Forces, 2017', Bulletin of the Atomic Scientists, vol. 73, no. 1, pp. 48–57, http://thebulletin.org/2017/january/united-states-nuclear-forces-201710380.

[5] Amy F. Woolf, 'U.S. Strategic Nuclear Forces: Background, Developments, and Issues', Congressional Research Service, RL33640, 10 February 2017, https://www.fas.org/sgp/crs/nuke/RL33640.pdf.

[6] Congressional Budget Office, 'Estimated Budgetary Impacts of Alternative Levels of Strategic Forces', 18 March 1998, www.cbo.gov/sites/default/files/cbofiles/ftpdocs/3xx/doc392/altforce.pdf; Department of Defense, 'Remarks by Deputy Secretary of Defense Carter at the Aspen Security Forum at Aspen, Colorado', 18 July 2013, http://archive.defense.gov/Transcripts/Transcript.aspx?TranscriptID=5277.

[7] Sydney J. Freedberg Jr, 'New ICBMs Could Cost Way Above $85B: CAPE'S Morin', Breaking Defense, 22 September 2016, http://breakingdefense.com/2016/09/new-icbms-could-cost-way-above-85b-capes-morin/.

[8] See Congressional Budget Office, 'An Analysis of the Navy's Fiscal Year 2014 Shipbuilding Plan', 18 October 2013, http://www.cbo.gov/publication/44655; and Jason Sherman, 'Navy Estimates $14.5B Tab for Lead Ohio-Class Replacement Submarine', Inside Defense, 18 March 2015, https://insidedefense.com/inside-pentagon/navy-estimates-145b-tab-lead-ohio-class-replacement-submarine.

[9] Jeff Tolleson, 'U.S. Warheads to Get a Facelift', Nature, vol. 497, 7 May 2013.

[10] Hans M. Kristensen, 'W80-1 Warhead Selected For New Nuclear Cruise Missile', Federation of American Scientists, 10 Oct 2014, https://fas.org/blogs/security/2014/10/w80-1_lrso/.

11 Department of Energy, 'Fiscal Year 2016 Stockpile Stewardship and Management Plan', March 2015, https://nnsa.energy.gov/sites/default/files/FY16SSMP_FINAL%20 3_16_2015_reducedsize.pdf.

12 The FY2016 National Defense Authorization Act states that a modern, responsive infrastructure, which includes the capability to produce 50–80 pits per year, is a national-security priority.

13 Union of Concerned Scientists, 'Making Smart Security Choices: The Future of the U.S. Nuclear Weapons Complex', October 2013, revised March 2014, http://www.ucsusa.org/sites/default/files/legacy/assets/documents/nwgs/nuclear-weapons-complex-report.pdf.

14 Union of Concerned Scientists, 'Making Smart Security Choices', p. 12.

15 Robert Alvarez, 'Y-12: Poster Child for a Dysfunctional Nuclear Weapons Complex', Bulletin of the Atomic Scientists, 4 August 2014, http://thebulletin.org/y-12-poster-child-dysfunctional-nuclear-weapons-complex7361.

Chapter Two

1 US Department of Defense, 'Nuclear Posture Review Report', April 2010, p. viii, http://www.defense.gov/Portals/1/features/defenseReviews/NPR/2010_Nuclear_Posture_Review_Report.pdf.

2 White House, 'Fact Sheet: Nuclear Weapons Employment Strategy of the United States', 19 June 2013, www.whitehouse.gov/the-press-office/2013/06/19/fact-sheet-nuclear-weapons-employment-strategy-united-states.

3 Charles L. Glaser, Analyzing Strategic Nuclear Policy (Princeton, NJ: Princeton University Press, 1990).

4 The exception to this is that 250 Minuteman III missiles currently configured for the Mk21 (SERV) re-entry vehicles with the larger and more modern 300-kilton W87 warhead cannot carry multiple warheads. However, the re-entry vehicles could be replaced with the Mk12-A re-entry vehicle to carry three 335-kilton W78 warheads.

5 Kris Osborn, 'B-2 Bomber Set to Receive Massive Upgrade', 25 June 2014, http://dodbuzz.com/2014/06/25/b-2-bomber-set-to-receive-massive-upgrade/. A 30,000-pound (13,607kg) conventional bomb has the explosive power equal to 0.015 kilotons.

6 Loren Thompson, 'B-3: The Inside Story of America's Next Bomber', Forbes, 2 September 2015, http://www.forbes.com/sites/lorenthompson/2015/09/02/b-3-the-inside-story-of-americas-next-bomber/.

7 These include the B61-12 and the W80-4. In addition, hundreds of ICBM and SLBM warheads could be used in the 'primary only' mode to greatly reduce their explosive yield, if required.

8 This force structure contains such a degree of overkill that the use of far less than one-tenth of its destructive force defies credibility. This is because exploding 100 modern nuclear warheads in urban or semi-urban areas would kill millions of people in the United States, even if no warheads detonated on the US homeland. The

atmospheric pollution that would result from such an attack would cause a 'nuclear winter' that would collapse global food production, putting 2bn people at risk of starvation. See Alan Robock and Owen Brian Toon, 'Self-Assured Destruction: The Climate Impacts of Nuclear War', Bulletin of the Atomic Scientists, 1 September 2012, http://thebulletin.org/2012/september/self-assured-destruction-climate-impacts-nuclear-war.

9   These include the B61-12 and the W80-4. In addition, hundreds of ICBM and SLBM warheads could be used in the 'primary only' mode to greatly reduce their explosive yield, if required.

10 'Lowering Nuclear Risks: An Interview With Former Defense Secretary William Perry', Arms Control Today, vol. 46, no. 1, January–February 2016, http://www.armscontrol.org/ACT/2016_0102/Features/Interviews/Lowering-Nuclear-Risks-An-Interview-With-Former-Defense-Secretary-William-Perry.

11 These include the B61-12. In addition, hundreds of SLBM warheads could be used in the 'primary only' mode to

greatly reduce their explosive yield, if required.

12 The Virginia-class submarines would have to carry a modified version of the Trident-II missile to fit in the VPM tubes that are slightly shorter than the tubes for the existing Trident II LE missile. If planning and development began now, a modified missile could be available by 2025. Lockheed Martin and Alliant Techsystems completed initial work on submarine-launched intermediate-range ballistic missiles in 2005 but the concept was not pursued. See http://www.globalsecurity.org/wmd/systems/slirbm.htm.

13 Dave Majumdar, 'The U.S. Navy's Dangerous Nuclear Attack Submarine Shortage', National Interest, 23 May 2016, http://nationalinterest.org/blog/the-buzz/the-us-navys-dangerous-nuclear-attack-submarine-shortage-16304.

14 These include the B61-12 and the W80-4. In addition, hundreds of ICBM and SLBM warheads could be used in the 'primary only' mode to greatly reduce their explosive yield, if required.

Chapter Three

1   See Robert Jervis, The Meaning of the Nuclear Revolution (Ithaca, NY: Cornell University Press, 1989).

2   US Department of Defense, 'Report on Nuclear Employment Strategy of the United States Specified in Section 491 of 10 U.S.C.', 2013, p. 3, http://www.globalsecurity.org/wmd/library/policy/dod/us-nuclear-employment-strategy.pdf.

3   A detailed description of the new military capabilities of the B61-12

nuclear weapon is provided by Hans M. Kristensen of the Federation of American Scientists. See Hans M. Kristensen, 'General Confirms Enhanced Targeting Capabilities of B61-12 Nuclear Bomb', Federation of American Scientists, 23 January 2014, http://fas.org/blogs/security/2014/01/b61capability/.

4   Matthew Bodner, 'Kremlin Threatens Response to U.S. Nuclear Bomb

Deployment in Germany', *Moscow Times*, 23 September 2015, http://www.themoscowtimes.com/business/article/kremlin-threatens-response-to-us-nuclear-bomb-deployment-in-germany/535106.html.

5   Zachary Keck, 'America and Russia Test New Tactical Nuclear Missiles', *National Interest*, 13 July 2015, http://nationalinterest.org/blog/the-buzz/america-russia-test-new-tactical-nuclear-missiles-13319.

6   Stephen Young, 'Commentary: US Is More Secure Without New, Nuclear-armed Cruise Missile', *Defense News*, 13 January 2016, http://www.defensenews.com/story/defense/commentary/2016/01/13/why-is-the-obama-administration-promoting-the-the-long-range-standoff-weapon/78693312/.

7   Hans M. Kristensen, 'Forget LRSO; JASSM-ER Can Do The Job', Federation of American Scientists, 16 December 2015, https://fas.org/blogs/security/2015/12/lrso-jassm/.

8   Michael R. Gordon, 'U.S. Says Russia Tested Cruise Missile, Violating Treaty', *New York Times*, 28 July 2014, http://www.nytimes.com/2014/07/29/world/europe/us-says-russia-tested-cruise-missile-in-violation-of-treaty.html.

9   James E. Doyle, 'Keeping Russia's Missiles Away from Europe', *National Interest*, 1 October 2015, http://nationalinterest.org/feature/keeping-russias-missiles-away-europe-13979.

10 J.D. Crouch, 'Special Briefing on the Nuclear Posture Review', 9 January 2002, https://fas.org/sgp/news/2002/01/npr-briefing.html; Donald H. Rumsfeld, unclassified cover letter for Nuclear Posture Review report to Congress, 9 January 2002, https://fas.org/sgp/news/2002/01/npr-foreword.html.

11 James M. Acton, 'Reclaiming Strategic Stability', 5 February 2013, Strategic Studies Institute, http://carnegieendowment.org/2013/02/05/reclaiming-strategic-stability/fkp6.

12 Forrest E. Morgan, *Crisis Stability and Long-Range Strike: A Comparative Analysis of Fighters, Bombers, and Missiles* (Santa Monica, CA: RAND Corporation, 2013), http://www.rand.org/pubs/monographs/MG1258.html.

13 James M. Acton, 'A New High-Speed Arms Race', 21 November 2014, Independent Military Review, http://carnegieendowment.org/2014/11/21/new-high-speed-arms-race/hwi7.

14 The National Missile Defense programme based in Alaska and California, which is designed to protect the United States from a North Korean or Iranian missile attack, continues to be unreliable. This was the conclusion of a Government Accountability Office report on missile defence concerning the GMD system. See US Government Accountability Office, 'Missile Defense', 17 February 2016, http://www.gao.gov/assets/680/675263.pdf.

15 Aria Bendix, 'U.S. Conducts Successful Missile Defense Test', *Atlantic*, 30 May 2017, https://www.theatlantic.com/news/archive/2017/05/us-conducts-successful-missile-defense-test/528591/.

16 Jaganath Sankaran, 'Missile Defense Against Iran Without Threatening Russia', *Arms Control Today*, vol. 43, no. 9, 4 November 2013, http://www.armscontrol.org/print/6020; David Larter, 'U.S. Missile Defense Site in Romania Starts Up, Angering Russia', *Navy Times*, 17 December 2015, http://www.navytimes.com/story/

military/2015/12/17/romania-missile-shield-capable-putin-russia-navy/77478556/.

[17] Kingston Reif, 'U.S. Nuclear Modernization Programs', Arms Control Association, August 2017, https://www.armscontrol.org/factsheets/USNuclearModernization.

[18] Hans M. Kristensen, Matthew McKinzie and Theodore A. Postol, 'How US Nuclear Force Modernization is Undermining Strategic Stability: The Burst-Height Compensating Super-Fuze', Bulletin of the Atomic Scientists, 1 March 2017, http://thebulletin.org/how-us-nuclear-force-modernization-undermining-strategic-stability-burst-height-compensating-super10578.

[19] Bruce Blair, 'Could U.S.–Russia Tensions Go Nuclear?', Politico Magazine, 27 November 2015, http://www.politico.com/magazine/story/2015/11/russia-us-tensions-nuclear-cold-war-213395#ixzz3yJZCZboo.

[20] Gregory Kulacki, 'China's Military Calls for Putting its Nuclear Forces on Alert', Union of Concerned Scientists, January 2016, http://www.ucsusa.org/sites/default/files/attach/2016/02/China-Hair-Trigger-full-report.pdf.

[21] 'Sarmat', Deagel, 7 April 2017, http://www.deagel.com/Ballistic-Missiles/Sarmat_a002919001.aspx.

[22] Franz-Stefan Gady, 'China Tests New Rail-Mobile Missile Capable of Hitting all of US', Diplomat, 5 January 2016, http://thediplomat.com/2016/01/china-tests-new-rail-mobile-missile-capable-of-hitting-all-of-us/.

[23] Former secretary of defense William Perry has recommended such a step. See William J. Perry and Andy Weber, 'Mr. President, Kill the New Cruise Missile', Washington Post, 15 October 2015, https://www.washingtonpost.com/opinions/mr-president-kill-the-new-cruise-missile/2015/10/15/e3e2807c-6ecd-11e5-9bfe-e59f5e244f92_story.html?utm_term=.c495e7ec744d.

[24] Malcolm Davis, 'Russia's New RS-28 Sarmat ICBM: A U.S. Missile Defense Killer?', National Interest, 15 February 2017, http://nationalinterest.org/blog/the-buzz/russias-new-rs-28-sarmat-icbm-us-missile-defense-killer-19464.

[25] 'Nuclear Arms Control and Disarmament Approaches in a Changed Security Environment', remarks by Frank A. Rose, Oslo, Norway, 30 September 2015, https://2009-2017.state.gov/t/avc/rls/2015/247623.htm.

[26] Sam LaGrone, 'Successful SM-6 Ballistic Missile Defense Test Set To Expand Capability of U.S. Guided Missile Fleet', USNI News, 4 August 2015, http://news.usni.org/2015/08/04/successful-sm-6-ballistic-missile-defense-test-set-to-expand-capability-of-u-s-guided-missile-fleet.

[27] Michael R. Gordon, 'Russia Has Deployed Missile Barred by Treaty, U.S. General Tells Congress', New York Times, 8 March 2017, https://www.nytimes.com/2017/03/08/us/politics/russia-inf-missile-treaty.html?mcubz=1&_r=0.

[28] Ministry of Foreign Affairs of the Russian Federation, 'Reply by Foreign Ministry Spokesperson Maria Zakharova to a Media Question on US Claims Regarding Russia's Reluctance to Continue Nuclear Disarmament', 5 April 2016, http://www.mid.ru/en/foreign_policy/news/-/asset_publisher/cKNonkJE02Bw/content/id/2207980.

29 US Department of State, 'Treaty Between the United States of America and the Russian Federation on Further Reduction and Limitation of Strategic Offensive Arms (START II)', 3 January 1993, http://www.state.gov/t/avc/trty/102887.htm.

30 Lani Miyoshi Sanders, Sharon M. DeLand and Arian L. Pregenzer, 'Integrating Nuclear Weapons Stockpile Management and Nuclear Arms Control Objectives to Enable Significant Stockpile Reductions', *Nonproliferation Review*, vol. 10, no. 3, 2010, pp. 475–89, http://www.tandfonline.com/doi/abs/10.1080/10736700.2010.516997.

31 'SSGN "Tactical Trident" Subs: Special Forces and Super Strike', *Defense Industry Daily*, 9 December 2011, http://www.defenseindustrydaily.com/ssgn-tactical-trident-subs-special-forces-and-super-strike-01764/.

Chapter Four

1 US Department of Defense, 'Report on Nuclear Employment Strategy of the United States Specified in Section 491 of 10 U.S.C.', 2013, p. 2, http://www.globalsecurity.org/wmd/library/policy/dod/us-nuclear-employment-strategy.pdf.

2 Defense Science Board, 'Seven Defense Priorities for the New Administration', December 2016, http://www.acq.osd.mil/dsb/reports/2010s/Seven_Defense_Priorities.pdf; Matthew Bunn et al., 'Preventing Nuclear Terrorism: Continuous Improvement or Dangerous Decline?', Project on Managing the Atom, Belfer Center for Science and International Affairs, March 2016, http://www.belfercenter.org/sites/default/files/files/publication/PreventingNuclearTerrorism-Web%202.pdf.

3 Matthew Bunn, Nicholas Roth and William H. Tobey, 'Cutting Too Deep: The Obama Administration's Proposals for Nuclear Security Spending Reductions', Project on Managing the Atom, Belfer Center for Science and International Affairs, 30 July 2014, http://belfercenter.ksg.harvard.edu/files/budgetpaper%20WEB.pdf.

4 Center for Arms Control and Non-Proliferation, 'Fiscal Year 2017 Defense Spending Request Briefing Book', February 2016, p. 7, https://armscontrolcenter.org/wp-content/uploads/2016/05/FY-17-Briefing-Book.pdf. See also Erica Fein, 'The Nuclear Terror Threat and Funding Mismatch', *Huffington Post*, 14 April 2016, http://m.huffpost.com/us/entry/the-nuclear-terror-threat_b_9696164.html.

5 See Kingston Reif, 'First Trump Budget Continues Unnecessary and Unsustainable Nuclear Weapons Plans', Arms Control Now, 7 June 2017, https://www.armscontrol.org/blog/2017-06-07/first-trump-budget-continues-unnecessary-unsustainable-nuclear-weapons-plans; Department of Energy, 'FY 2018 Congressional Budget Request, Volume 1, National Nuclear Security Administration: Federal Salaries and Expenses Weapons Activities', May 2017, https://energy.gov/sites/prod/files/2017/05/f34/FY2018BudgetVolume1_1.pdf.

6 'Report of the Secretary of Defense Task Force on DoD Nuclear Weapons

Management: Phase I: The Air Force's Nuclear Mission', September 2008, http://www.globalsecurity.org/wmd/library/report/2008/nuclear-weapons_phase-1_2008-09-10.htm.

7 Hans M. Kristensen, 'USAF Report: Most Nuclear Weapon Sites in Europe Do Not Meet US Security Requirements', Federation of American Scientists, 19 June 2008, https://fas.org/blogs/security/2008/06/usaf-report-most-nuclear-weapon-sites-in-europe-do-not-meet-us-security-requirements/; US Air Force, 'Air Force Blue Ribbon Review of Nuclear Weapons Policies and Procedures', 8 February 2008, http://fas.org/nuke/guide/usa/doctrine/usaf/BRR-2008.pdf.

8 Hans M. Kristensen, 'US Nuclear Weapons Site in Europe Breached', 4 February 2010, Federation of American Scientists, https://fas.org/blogs/security/2010/02/kleinebrogel/.

9 'Reports: US Nuclear "Upgrades" in Europe', 23 September 2015, Deutsche Welle, www.dw.com/en/reports-us-nuclear-upgrades-in-europe/a-18731756.

10 Timothy Farnsworth, 'Study Sees Cyber Risk for U.S. Arsenal', Arms Control Today, vol. 43, no. 3, 2 April 2013, https://www.armscontrol.org/act/2013_04/Study-Sees-Cyber-Risk-for-US-Arsenal; Bruce Blair, 'Could Terrorists Launch America's Nuclear Missiles?', Time, 11 November 2010, http://content.time.com/time/nation/article/0,8599,2030685,00.html; Franz-Stefan Gady, 'Could Cyber Attacks Lead to Nuclear War?', Diplomat, 4 May 2015, http://thediplomat.com/2015/05/could-cyber-attacks-lead-to-nuclear-war/.

11 John M. Donnelly, 'Exclusive: Aging Helicopters Could Make U.S. Nukes Vulnerable to Terrorists', 29 February 2016, http://www.rollcall.com/news/exclusive_aging_helicopters_could_make_us_nukes_vulnerable_to_terrorists-246074-1.html.

12 Jenn Rowell, 'Lawmakers: New Helicopters Needed Now for ICBM Security', Great Falls Tribune, 29 June 2016, http://www.greatfallstribune.com/story/news/local/2016/06/29/lawmakers-new-helicopters-needed-now-icbm-security/86536578/.

13 Major-General Robertus C.N. Remkes, 'The Security of NATO Nuclear Weapons: Issues and Implications', in Reducing Nuclear Risks in Europe: A Framework for Action, Nuclear Threat Initiative, 17 November 2011, pp. 66–75, http://www.nti.org/media/pdfs/NTI_Framework_Chpt3.pdf?_=13227016952011:66.

14 The estimated savings of Option 1 (streamlined triad) are based on calculations contained in the interactive cost model created by the Center for American Progress. See Center for American Progress, 'The Future of the U.S. Nuclear Arsenal', 2016, https://interactives.americanprogress.org/future-of-nukes/#.

15 Matthew Bunn et al., 'Preventing Nuclear Terrorism'.

16 Center for Arms Control and Non-Proliferation, 'Press Release: FY 17 Budget Cuts Key Non-Proliferation Programs', 9 February 2016, http://armscontrolcenter.org/press-release-fy-17-budget-cuts-key-non-proliferation-programs/.

17 Andrew Futter, 'Cyber Threats and Nuclear Weapons: New Questions for Command and Control, Security and Strategy', RUSI, 15 July 2016,

https://rusi.org/publication/occasional-papers/cyber-threats-and-nuclear-weapons-new-questions-command-and-control.

18   United Nations Office for Disarmament Affairs, 'Treaty on the Non-Proliferation of Nuclear Weapons (NPT)', https://www.un.org/disarmament/wmd/nuclear/npt/text/.

19   James E. Doyle, 'NPT Disarmament Obligations and Nuclear Myth-Busting', Arms Control Now, 24 April 2015, https://www.armscontrol.org/blog/ArmsControlNow/2014-04-24/NPT-Disarmament-Obligations-and-Nuclear-Myth-Busting; Acronym Institute for Disarmament Diplomacy, '2000 NPT Review Conference, Final Document (13 Steps)', 20 May 2000, http://www.acronym.org.uk/old/official-and-govt-documents/2000-npt-review-conference-final-document-13-steps; Australian Department of Foreign Affairs and Trade, '2010 NPT Review Conference 64-point Action Plan', http://dfat.gov.au/international-relations/security/non-proliferation-disarmament-arms-control/policies-agreements-treaties/treaty-on-the-non-proliferation-of-nuclear-weapons/Pages/2010-npt-review-conference-64-point-action-plan.aspx.

20   William J. Perry et al., America's Strategic Posture: The Final Report of the Congressional Commission on the Strategic Posture of the United States (Washington DC: United States Institute of Peace, 2009), p. xi, http://www.usip.org/sites/default/files/America's_Strategic_Posture_Auth_Ed.pdf.

21   William J. Perry et al., America's Strategic Posture, p. x.

22   Jayantha Dhanapala and Sergio Duarte, 'Is There a Future for the NPT?', Arms Control Today, vol. 45, no. 6, July–

August 2015, http://www.armscontrol.org/ACT/2015_0708/Features/Is-There-a-Future-for-the-NPT. See also Adam Mount, 'New Dawn for the NPT: The United States' Real Record on Proliferation', Foreign Affairs, 22 April 2015, https://www.foreignaffairs.com/articles/2015-04-22/new-dawn-npt.

23   Article VI of the NPT commits all state parties to 'pursue negotiations in good faith on effective measures relating to cessation of the nuclear arms race at an early date and to nuclear disarmament, and on a treaty on general and complete disarmament under strict and effective international control'. This article has since been clarified by the treaty-review process to apply specifically to nuclear disarmament.

24   US Department of Defense, 'Nuclear Posture Review Report', April 2010, p. vi, http://www.defense.gov/Portals/1/features/defenseReviews/NPR/2010_Nuclear_Posture_Review_Report.pdf.

25   Australian Department of Foreign Affairs and Trade, '2010 NPT Review Conference 64-point Action Plan', http://dfat.gov.au/international-relations/security/non-proliferation-disarmament-arms-control/policies-agreements-treaties/treaty-on-the-non-proliferation-of-nuclear-weapons/Pages/2010-npt-review-conference-64-point-action-plan.aspx.

26   Vertical proliferation refers to the expansion of the arsenals of nuclear weapons in states that already possess them.

27   Adam Mount, 'Anticipatory Arms Control', Deep Cuts Working Paper, no. 7, June 2016, http://www.deepcuts.org/images/DeepCuts_WP6_Mount.pdf.

28   James Martin Center for Nonproliferation Studies, '2014 NPT

Action Plan Monitoring Report', 23 April 2014, www.nonproliferation. org/2014-npt-action-plan-monitoring-report/.

[29] The interoperable-warhead plan is described in Chapter One.

[30] Tom Collina, 'NNSA's "3+2" Nuclear Warhead Plan Does Not add Up', *Arms Control Association Issue Briefs*, vol. 5, issue 6, 6 May 2014, https://

www.armscontrol.org/issuebriefs/ NNSAs-3%202-Nuclear-Warhead-Plan-Does-Not-Add-Up%20.

[31] Lisbeth Gronlund, 'Bad Math on New Nuclear Weapons: The Costs of the 3+2 Plan Outweigh Its Benefits', Union of Concerned Scientists, October 2015, http://www.ucsusa.org/sites/ default/files/attach/2015/11/Bad-Math-Nuclear-Weapons-3-Plus-2.pdf.

Chapter Five

[1] James Drew, 'USAF Calls for Nuclear Debate as Fiscal Realities Set in', FlightGlobal, 12 February 2016, https:// www.flightglobal.com/news/articles/ usaf-calls-for-nuclear-debate-as-fiscal-realities-se-421883/.

[2] Lawrence J. Korb and Adam Mount, 'Setting Priorities for Nuclear Modernization', Center for American Progress, 3 February 2016, https:// www.americanprogress.org/issues/ security/report/2016/02/03/130431/ setting-priorities-for-nuclear-modernization/; Jeremiah Gertler, 'The Air Force Aviation Investment Challenge', Congressional Research Service, 17 December 2015, https:// www.fas.org/sgp/crs/weapons/ R44305.pdf.

[3] Navy officials have stated that if the Navy does not receive the supplemental (and currently unbudgeted) funding that it is requesting for the *Ohio*-class-replacement programme, it would need to eliminate from its 30-year shipbuilding plan a notional total of 32 other ships, including eight *Virginia*-class attack submarines, eight destroyers and 16 other combatant

ships. See Ronald O'Rourke, 'Navy Columbia Class (Ohio Replacement) Ballistic Missile Submarine (SSBN[X]) Program: Background and Issues for Congress', 12 May 2017, p. 30, https:// fas.org/sgp/crs/weapons/R41129.pdf.

[4] The estimated savings of the streamlined triad are based on calculations contained in the interactive cost model created by the Center for American Progress. See Center for American Progress, 'The Future of the U.S. Nuclear Arsenal', 2016, https:// interactives.americanprogress.org/ future-of-nukes/#.

[5] Todd Harrison, 'Defense Modernization Plans through the 2020s: Addressing the Bow Wave', Center for Strategic and International Studies, 27 January 2016, http:// csis.org/files/publication/160126_ Harrison_DefenseModernization_ Web.pdf.

[6] The estimated savings of the air–sea dyad are based on calculations contained in the interactive cost model created by the Center for American Progress. See Center for American Progress, 'The Future of the U.S. Nuclear Arsenal' 2016, https://

interactives.americanprogress.org/
future-of-nukes/#.

[7] David A. Shlapak and Michael
Johnson, 'Reinforcing Deterrence on
NATO's Eastern Flank: Wargaming the
Defense of the Baltics', RAND, 2016,
http://www.rand.org/content/dam/
rand/pubs/research_reports/RR1200/
RR1253/RAND_RR1253.synopsis.pdf.

[8] The estimated savings of the
dispersed maritime dyad are based on
calculations contained in the interactive
cost model created by the Center for
American Progress. See Center for
American Progress, 'The Future of the
U.S. Nuclear Arsenal' 2016, https://
interactives.americanprogress.org/
future-of-nukes/#.

Conclusions

[1] The US plans to buy at least 4,000
new *Tomahawk* land-attack missiles
(>1,600km range) and nearly 3,000
JASSM–ERs (>800km range) during
the next five years. See Ryan Maass,
'U.S. Navy Requests 4,000 Tomahawk
Cruise Missiles in Budget', UPI,
4 February 2016, http://www.upi.
com/Business_News/Security-
Industry/2016/02/04/US-Navy-
requests-4000-Tomahawk-cruise-
missiles-in-budget/1461454610038.

[2] 'Report on the Strategic Nuclear Forces
of the Russian Federation Pursuant to
Section 1240 of the National Defense
Authorization Act for Fiscal Year 2012',
https://fas.org/programs/ssp/nukes/
nuclearweapons/DOD2012_Russian
Nukes.pdf.

[3] Michael Klare, 'Playing a Game of
Chicken with Nuclear Strategy', War

is Boring, 7 November 2016, https://
warisboring.com/playing-a-game-
of-chicken-with-nuclear-strategy-
7baa0d5111e3#.ol6vwlu30.

[4] Hans M. Kristensen, 'DOD: Strategic
Stability Not Threatened Even by
Greater Russian Nuclear Forces',
Federation of American Scientists,
10 October 2012, https://fas.org/
blogs/security/2012/10/strategic
stability/.

[5] Hope Hodge Seck, 'Former SecDef:
Remove ICBMs From Nuclear
Triad', Military.com, 18 December 2015, http://www.military.com/
daily-news/2015/12/18/former-sec-
def-remove-icbms-from-nuclear-
triad.html; Mark Thompson, 'Triad
And True...', *Time*, 21 June 2013,
http://nation.time.com/2013/06/21/
triad-and-true/.

INDEX

 IISS ADELPHI BOOKS

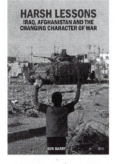

ADELPHI 461

Harsh Lessons: Iraq, Afghanistan
and the Changing Character
of War

Ben Barry

ISBN 978-1-138-06096-8

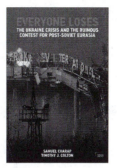

ADELPHI 460

Everyone Loses: The Ukraine
Crisis and the Ruinous Contest for
Post-Soviet Eurasia

Samuel Charap and Timothy J. Colton

ISBN 978-1-138-63308-7

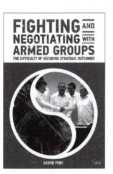

ADELPHI 459

**Fighting and Negotiating with
Armed Groups:** The Difficulty of
Securing Strategic Outcomes

Samir Puri

ISBN 978-1-138-23856-5

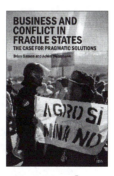

ADELPHI 457–458

**Business and Conflict in
Fragile States:** the Case for
Pragmatic Solutions

Achim Wennmann and Brian Ganson

ISBN 978-1-138-21397-5

For credit card orders call **+44 (0) 1264 343 071**
or e-mail **book.orders@tandf.co.uk**
Orders can also be placed at **www.iiss.org**

Routledge
Taylor & Francis Group

Adelphi books are published eight times a year by Routledge Journals, an imprint of Taylor & Francis, 4 Park Square, Milton Park, Abingdon, Oxfordshire OX14 4RN, UK.

A subscription to the institution print edition, ISSN 1944-5571, includes free access for any number of concurrent users across a local area network to the online edition, ISSN 1944-558X. Taylor & Francis has a flexible approach to subscriptions enabling us to match individual libraries' requirements. This journal is available via a traditional institutional subscription (either print with free online access, or online-only at a discount) or as part of our libraries, subject collections or archives. For more information on our sales packages please visit www.tandfonline.com/librarians_pricinginfo_journals.

2017 Annual Adelphi Subscription Rates			
Institution	£684	US$1,201	€1,013
Individual	£242	US$413	€330
Online only	£599	US$1,051	€886

Dollar rates apply to subscribers outside Europe. Euro rates apply to all subscribers in Europe except the UK and the Republic of Ireland where the pound sterling price applies. All subscriptions are payable in advance and all rates include postage. Journals are sent by air to the USA, Canada, Mexico, India, Japan and Australasia. Subscriptions are entered on an annual basis, i.e. January to December. Payment may be made by sterling cheque, dollar cheque, international money order, National Giro, or credit card (Amex, Visa, Mastercard).

For a complete and up-to-date guide to Taylor & Francis journals and books publishing programmes, and details of advertising in our journals, visit our website: **http://www.tandfonline.com.**

Ordering information:
USA/Canada: Taylor & Francis Inc., Journals Department, 530 Walnut Street, Suite 850, Philadelphia, PA 19106, USA. **UK/Europe/Rest of World:** Routledge Journals, T&F Customer Services, T&F Informa UK Ltd., Sheepen Place, Colchester, Essex, CO3 3LP, UK.

Advertising enquiries to:
USA/Canada: The Advertising Manager, Taylor & Francis Inc., 530 Walnut Street, Suite 850, Philadelphia, PA 19106, USA. Tel: +1 (800) 354 1420. Fax: +1 (215) 207 0050. **UK/Europe/Rest of World**: The Advertising Manager, Routledge Journals, Taylor & Francis, 4 Park Square, Milton Park, Abingdon, Oxfordshire OX14 4RN, UK. Tel: +44 (0) 20 7017 6000. Fax: +44 (0) 20 7017 6336.